S^{The}ection 8 Bible

Section 8 Housing Guide

Volume II

We're B-a-a-a-c-k!
*Just when tenants **thought** it was safe*
to go back inside their homes!

Michael McLean
Nick Cipriano

Formatted by: Sohail Liaqat

Cover Design by: JD Cover Designs

Other books by this author:

The Section 8 Bible Vol 1
The Section 8 Bible Vol 2
The Section 8 Bible Vol 3
The Bulletproof Lease
Metal Money
Section 8 Secrets

CONTENTS

PREFACE

We're back! It's been a year and a half since we ripped the tenants, the inspectors, and Section 8 a new ass and we're ready to do just that again! We will be holding nothing back! If you liked Volume I, you're gonna love Volume II!

Volume I was a feeler of sorts. We put out a great book and we also saw what we could get away with. This time around, we're gonna push it to the limit. In fact, we're gonna go over the limit and rip the roof off this Section 8 land lording business!

So sit down, get yourself a nice drink, a bag of popcorn, and get ready to laugh, learn, and save with the greatest landlord book ever written – The Section 8 Bible Volume II is finally here!!!

CHAPTER 1

WE'RE BACK

Wow! What a response is all I can say. It's been a year and a half since we released Volume I and we honestly didn't think we were going to get that kind of a response. I feel like a rock star with my fans anxiously awaiting our second album. Believe me, we are going to do our best not to disappoint you!

We thought we covered everything previously. A lot of you had asked some very good questions that we are going to answer here in Volume II. Some of you had some ridiculous questions that we will not be answering. I think that the more ridiculous questions came from tenants disguised as landlords. They must have clicked onto the website, read what the book was about, and then proceeded to blast me with questions like this: "I am also a Section 8 landlord and I don't agree with the way you treat your tenants! How could you be so mean and why would you eliminate things from your home that could be useful to your tenants?"

Now does that sound like a question from a real landlord? A real jackass for sure, but obviously not a real landlord (I said we had a tremendous response, not all of it was positive). On second thought, I think I will answer some ridiculous questions! The answer to "How could you be so mean?" is RESPECT! I've dedicated an entire chapter in this book to "Respect" including why you need it and how to get it. What we have found over the years is that tenants take kindness for weakness. It's weird but for some reason they take being stern and aggressive with them as a form of respect. The second, and last, ridiculous question I will be answering is "Why do you eliminate things that could be useful to your tenant?" Duh! Perhaps I love saving money. Maybe I like watching television on Saturday morning, rather than spending the day over at my tenant's house trying to free up the clogged garbage disposal. There is probably ten thousand ways I could answer this ridiculous question without getting it wrong but, the one answer I like the best—and you should all know it by now is, "You don't need it to pass inspection!!!"

Let me give you a quick rundown of what's going to be covered here in Volume II. We received thousands and thousands of great questions from other landlords. Not only did we receive questions, we received answers! A lot of landlords told me what they did to get around a certain roadblock and we intend to pass their story and solution along to you. Some landlords had wonderful ideas that we thought were brilliant. Others had some ideas that I had to scratch my head and say, "Is this guy a jerkoff or what?" You won't be reading any of those stories (although some are rather funny). I won't waste a minute of your time with stupid ideas from crazy landlords.

Stories, stories, stories!! I got the biggest feedback from some of the stories I told in Volume I. Most of you thought they were hysterical and wanted to hear more and more (I never knew I was such a funny guy). Well guess what? You're in luck. A lot has happened in a year and a half. We've got a few more good stories for ya. Here's a little taste.

Remember in Volume I when I said I never had to pull my gun? Well, my luck ran out and a situation presented itself. Obviously since you're reading Volume II, the situation worked out in my favor but, boy oh boy, you wanna talk about scary!

Remember when I talked about becoming friendly with the inspectors? Yeah, well, I got a story about how I became an enemy of one. And just like most of our stories, I'm gonna tell you what we did to come out on top!

"What have we been doing since we sold off our entire portfolio?" This is another question that a lot of you asked. I wish the answer could have been something like: "We hang out on Nick's yacht during the day, go golfing later in the afternoon, and at night we go out with one of our many young model girlfriends." Unfortunately, Nick didn't buy a yacht and we both hate golf, but the rest is true (we wish)!

Yeah, the lure of underpriced homes, high rent returns, and guaranteed rent came calling us back! Shortly after the sell-off, we purchased a package of 58 homes from a local Philadelphia landlord. Twenty-one of the homes were rented Section 8 and the rest were private rents. You know, that changed in a hurry! They are now all rented Section 8. There's a new sheriff in town, Mike and Nick! I'll get further into detail about what we're doing now and where we intend on going.

ELIMINATION! Ooohhh yeah, we found more shit to eliminate! That's right, the longer you hang around in this business the more shit bites you in the ass. On the other side of the coin, the more shit bites you in the ass, the more you can eliminate! We thought we had it all figured out. We thought we found everything in the house from the tip of the roof to the basement floor that we could possibly eliminate. We were wrong!

We found some more items on our own and some of you landlords out there dropped us an e-mail on what they eliminate! We'll give you the reason we eliminate it, we'll give you the reason they eliminate it.

Products! – There are some new products that we found out there that are cheaper than what we were using and last just as long if not longer. Nick's always shopping for new quality products and we'll give you a rundown of what's in his shopping cart. We'll tell you the how, when and where of when to use these products.

Organize! – Being and keeping organized is the only way to run your business. You cannot be successful unless you are organized. From day one, Nick and I have been just that. Think we're the kings of elimination? You should see us when it comes to organization! Hell, our toilets are even organized.

Organized toilets, tanks, and toilet seats

It's the only way to live and we are going to give you some ideas on how you can be more organized and stay that way. Don't be that landlord who has to dig through a shoebox with 55 sets of keys in it just to find the set you're looking for!

Finding properties! – Another question we received a lot of was, "How and where did you guys find all of those cheap properties?" That question was usually followed by, "How can you tell if you're in a bad neighborhood?"

When that question first came across my computer screen I laughed and thought, "What, is this guy joking? How the hell can you not know if you're in a bad neighborhood?" Then I received that question again and again. Put me in the middle of the block on an inner city street in Chicago, Detroit, Miami, etc. and I'll be able to tell you if you're in a good, bad, or really bad neighborhood! And guess what? I haven't even been to any of those cities! Then again, I was born in the city and I'm a very street smart guy. I know what to look for, who not to look at, and when to get my ass out of there.

I wasn't even thinking about a guy who lives in upstate New York who wants to come down into the city and start buying and renting some properties out. We're also gonna throw in some more "Street Smarts" tips to help you stay safe.

Since the real estate market started heating up, a lot of you country boys started coming out of the sticks and buying some inner city properties. Also, since the stock market slowed, a lot of you office 9 to 5-ers started purchasing properties and coming into the city on the weekend to work on them.

Nothing wrong with that...I think it's great! It keeps the housing market growing and rolling. Being in the office or the woods all that time, you might not have a lot of street in ya! You'd better get it quick because if the bum on the corner senses you don't have it, you're gonna become a target. With the tips in this chapter, we will eliminate the "Bum Bull's-eyes" from your back.

Duplexes and multi-family units! – The question of, "Do you guys get involved with multi-family units or duplexes?" was another repeated question. I'll tell you the answer right now is NO, NO WAY! In this chapter we're gonna tell you several reasons why we don't.

Rent Increases! – Surprisingly a lot of you out there aren't getting your rent increases. In this chapter, we're going to make sure you get 'em. It's your right to get an increase in rent every year. The utility companies can increase the water bill or the electric bill every year, the city can increase the taxes whenever they want to, but you can't increase the rent? That's bullshit! I've heard from landlords who have had the same tenant in their property for 10 or 12 years and still haven't received a rent increase. Let Section 8 try to pull that on us and they'll have a full-scale war on their hands.

If you don't fight for it, you ain't gonna get it! It's like everything else in life, if you don't put up a fight, the other guy will think he's right. We're gonna show you how to fight that greedy "Tenant Service Rep" for what is rightfully yours. That's why she's got the word "Tenant" in front of her title. She's not there to help you, believe me! Have you ever heard of a "Landlord Service Rep"? Me neither and you never will. That's why you've got to fight for yourself; become your own Rep. If you've got balls, you'll be a good one. Back down, you'll be a horrible one and won't see one rent increase. The squeaky wheel gets the oil and we're gonna show you how to make that wheel sound so damn squeaky, the Service Rep will think it's going to fall off the cart!

Knowing the Rule Book! – This book may be a Bible for Section 8 Landlords but it's not the most important book out there (oh my god, I can't believe I just said that). The rule book or book of HQS (Housing Quality Standards) is the book you should know from front to back. It won't save you as much cash as this book, but it will sure make your life easier when getting the property ready for inspection. In this chapter, I'll go over some of the rules that inspectors try to fail you on even though you may already be in good shape!

Evictions! – Another question we received a ton of was "How do you go about evicting a tenant?" Most states vary and it's all a bunch of bullshit! Once the rent goes past 30 days late you should be able to throw them out on their ass; 90% of the time they never catch up on the rent and the excuses get dumber and dumber. In this chapter, I'm going to give you a couple ideas of how to stay out of the courtroom altogether!

Management Companies! – Another heavily asked question! Most of you wanted to know if we were for or against them. Others wanted to know what would be a fair price to pay a management company to manage your properties. The answer to #2 also answers #1. "I wouldn't know what would be a fair price to pay someone to manage my rentals. I have never done it, nor would I!" It's something that can be done rather easily, even if you can't drive a nail.

Here's how easy it works. If a tenant calls and says her hot water heater broke, pick up the phone book and call a couple of plumbers. Get the best price possible and have it installed. Let's say it cost $500 for everything.

Now, here's what a management company will do. They'll pick up the phone, call a couple of plumbers and get the best price. Then they'll add 200 bucks to that price and hit you with the bill. Now you're paying $700 instead of $500. Don't be a sucker! You don't have to know any trade skills...you just have to know how to use the phone book and have some balls.

Truth be known, the guy who owns the management company probably doesn't even know how to install a water heater. I'll also add a couple more reasons why I don't use management companies. I'm sure there are some good ones out there, but I believe it's something you can handle on your own!

Free Money! – Could it really be true? Or is that guy with the commercial and the question marks all over his green suit truly an idiot? Over the years, Nick and I have tried and applied to receive several different grants. Winterization, Low Income Housing, Roofing and Heating upgrades for Low Income Landlords, etc.; were we successful? Did we receive a piece of the "Free Money Pie"? The answer, yes and no! Read this chapter and you'll find out why.

Garages! Many of you who have garages on your property asked the same question, "What should we be doing with them?" There are a couple of different answers but what they all boil down to is, "Don't let your tenant have access to them!!!"

Garages and tenants don't mix!

That is, unless you want to rent a 30 or 40-yard dumpster to clean them out once your tenant moves. They'll pack them so tight with crap from front to back, you won't be able to fit a toothpick in there let alone get the door open. In this chapter, we will tell you several different ways to prevent this from happening.

Shop on Wheels! – We told you in Volume I about our stake body and how much time it saved us. Well, we purchased another vehicle that saves twice as much time! Not only does it save time, it saves man hours and gas. What is it? How much did it cost? All of those questions will be answered in this chapter.

Playing Dirty! – Every landlord has had that tenant from hell! I don't care if you're renting Section 8, commercial, vacation homes, $5,000 per month condos, etc. It happens. Follow our lead and 95% of the time we will keep you out of the courtroom. Four percent of the time you'll come to some kind of agreement in court, lick your wounds, cut your losses, and get your investment up and rented again. One percent of the time you'll meet that "Tenant or Judge from Hell." Either the tenant has been in and out of court so many times that they know every angle to bide themselves more time, or you get that judge that thinks you owe your poor tenant a living.

Now, you can either eat shit or start "Playing Dirty." Not that I've ever done it (wink), but I know two local Philadelphia landlords that are great at "Playing Dirty." Their names are Ike MacLane and Rick Cipranni and in this chapter, they'll tell you how to fight fire with fire.

Rule Changes! – There have been some major code and rule changes since we released Volume I and we are going to get into the major changes. Section 8 is always trying to come up with some new hoops for us landlords to jump through. We're not going to show you how to jump through them; we're going to show you how to simply walk around them!

Rules are made to be broken and we are the kings of breaking rules. Do you know why we're the kings of breaking rules? Because we do it legally! That's right, we break the rules legally. Want to write a new rule or throw up a barrier because you don't like the way we're doing something? Go right ahead. We'll figure out a way to come through the back door. We're rule book invincible! Tell us we need a railing going down the basement steps, I'll screw a 2" × 4" to the wall and call it a railing. Tell me that's not good enough. I'll screw a railing to the top of the 2" × 4." You ain't gonna beat us! No how, no way! The inspectors get up at 7 o'clock in the morning; we get up at six. The inspectors hate their job, we love this shit! We'll out smart, outthink and out work every inspector in the field, then we pass the info along to you! We'll let you know what we did to beat them, and we'll let you know what you can do to beat them. We are sort of the guinea pigs, if you will. We'll throw shit against the wall and if it sticks, we'll put it in our book.

That's why you loved Volume I and I know that you're going to love Volume II as well. I know I have to stop blowing my own horn here and start passing on some useful information (wow, has the success of Volume I gone to my head or what?).

All right, all right! I think I've given you a pretty good idea of what Volume II is going to be about so let's get started. Sit back, relax, and let's get ready to laugh, learn, and save some cash!!

CHAPTER 2

PLAYING DIRTY

I'm coming out swinging! I'm gonna jump right into the chapter that I think could very well be the best I've ever written. Let's see if you agree.

It's finally happened. You've run into that tenant from hell! You have done everything possible to get this low life out of your life, but some jackass judge says, "Uh uh, not so fast." He or she either gives the tenant an incredible amount of time, like perhaps 90 days to find another place to move or, worse yet, tells you you're wrong and denies the eviction all together!

As long as I live, I'll never get it. If you own the property and you don't want this bum living there any longer, how can an eviction be denied? I wish I had the answer, but I don't. It's ridiculous! It is lawyers who have never owned rental properties and never will, making up laws to protect free-loading, destructive tenants. You can either sit back and take it, (while your tenant laughs hysterically in your face after the verdict), or you can start "Playing Dirty!"

There are a lot of things I don't like in life, but some stand out more than others. One is losing money and the other is a tenant laughing in my face like she just won the lottery. After the judge tells them that they won, you would think that the judge issued them the deed to the house. Boy, oh boy, they are on cloud nine!

Meanwhile, you're ready to blow a 50 amp fuse! You're fantasizing about charging across the courtroom floor and smashing one of those nice, heavy wooden chairs over your tenant's head! Then, like Jackie Chan, leaping over the bench with what's left of the chair and playing a tune on "your honor's" head. Then somebody pinches you and you realize it was all a wonderful dream. However, when you awake, you are still stuck in your horrible nightmare with your ecstatic tenant who is now dancing out the courtroom door. It's time to start "Playing Dirty."

Fortunately, we know a lot of street smart landlords who are pretty good at playing dirty. Revenge is served best on a cold plate, but don't let it get too cold. The colder the plate gets, the longer your tenant stays. Even though you lost in court, don't forget what you were originally fighting for. For some reason or another you wanted this lowlife out of your life and just because somebody said, "No, I sentence you to put up with another year or more of this tenant's nonsense," doesn't mean you have to sit back and take it. Let me tell you a couple of ways my buddies Ike and Rick helped speed their tenant's thought process.

It was the summer of 1998 and man was it hot. Philly was caught up in one of those heat waves where it hit 100 degrees about five days in a row. Ike told me that whenever he drove by a certain one of his rental properties, the temperature in his truck would go up to 140 degrees... with the A/C on! He wasn't sure if it was from the steam coming off his head or his blood pressure doubling...but whatever the reason, it wasn't good.

Ya see, the tenant living in the property had failed their annual Section 8 inspection because they didn't have any gas on in the unit. Not that Ike did anything wrong, the tenant just felt like spending her utility check on something other than her utilities. Section 8 didn't pay Ike for the five weeks that the gas was off, and the tenant said she wasn't reimbursing him for the 5 weeks rent either. Naturally, Ike filed for eviction and went to court expecting an easy victory. Wrong!

The lying tenant made up a bogus story that she smelled gas coming from the heater. She didn't want anything to blow up so she just didn't pay the gas bill in hopes that the gas company would come out and shut it off. Never did she call Ike or the gas company. She just felt like not paying the bill, this would be the quickest way to eliminate the "phantom" gas leak.

Well, guess what? The judge bought it, eviction denied! The judge felt the tenant was credible and if you can believe this, "commended" her on her safety, no bullshit! That's when Rick stood up and said, "She doesn't need gas for the heater because its summertime and I'll lay you odds she doesn't need gas for the stove because she probably hasn't cooked a meal since Christmas!" Well, that's when the judge ordered Ike and Rick out of the courtroom...immediately!

If Rick wanted to elaborate a little more, he could have said she doesn't need a gas stove because she has a rusty barrel out front that is cut in half and filled with charcoal.

Barbeque barrell – also known as a tenant's stove when gas is turned off.

Whenever she lights it, Philadelphia International Airport has to re- route its planes and Indians try to answer her back! I won't even get into why she doesn't need gas for hot water!

Anyway, back to Ike and the heat wave. When he rode past the house, the tenant was out front. She looked at him with a big smile and then, bam! Up came her middle finger. Enough was enough. That night at about 3 o'clock in the morning, Ike parked about a block away from the property. He told me that even at three in the morning, it was still about 90 degrees as he walked up the alley towards the back of the property.

What did Ike do when he got to the back of the property? He pulled the electric meter! That's right; he just yanked the whole meter out of the socket.

What electric meter looked like before Ike got to it.

What meter looked like after Ike was finished with it!

I don't know if you know how hot a Philly row home with a black tar roof can get, but I imagine that by 4 o'clock in the morning, after the A/C was off for an hour, his tenant and anyone else in the house woke up in a puddle of sweat!

There was Mrs. Middle Finger, chillin' in the house that she owed rent on and then wham. "That's the night that the lights went out in Georgia!" You can live without gas, huh? Let's see if you can do without electric.

The next morning when Ike got into his office, he thought he would have had 55 calls from Mrs. Middle Finger...he had none! Two days went by and still no calls. He sent one of his workers up the alley and still the meter had not been replaced. Finally, on the third day, the phone rang while Ike was in his office:

Ike, "Hello."

Tenant, "Ike, you mother-fucker, I want my electric meter back!" she screamed.

"I don't know what you're talking about."

"Yes, you do, you son of a bitch, you took my electric meter," she insisted.Ike said, "Look, I didn't take anything. Call the electric company, not me. You didn't call me when you smelled gas so don't call me when you don't have electric."

"I did call them but I'm behind on the bill so they ain't coming out here."

Well, with that reply, Ike's ears stood up. The reason it took the woman three days to call him is because she assumed the electric company had cut her off. Not only did Ike do the electric company a favor, this fool just gave out some vital information which down the line could be very useful to use against her.

"Well, maybe the electric company took your meter."

"I talked to them and they said they don't do that." Then it was time for the tenant to try and play games. "Anyway, I got a picture of you taking my meter."

Number one, Ike has been in the tenant's home several times and knows that the tenant probably doesn't own a camera and if she did, it's either lost, broken, or out of film.

"That's nice, send it into the Daily News and tell them to put my picture on the front page. Goodbye!"

As quickly as Ike had hung up the phone, he was on his way down to the Section 8 office to have a little talk with the tenant's Service Rep and the Head of Inspections. First, he told the Head of Inspections that he wanted an "emergency inspection" set up for the following day. The reason was that the tenant was living in the property with no electric. Then he proceeded to walk over to the tenant's Service Rep and blow the whistle that the tenant isn't paying her electric bill which, of course, is a good enough reason to revoke her benefits and package.

The next day, Ike met the inspector outside the property. The tenant answered the door and the inspector told her that he was here for an emergency landlord inspection. "What for?" she asked.

"Well, ma'am, we are here to see if you have electric on in the unit."

"No, because that bastard stole my meter," she said pointing at Ike.

"I'm not here for accusations ma'am. I'm here to check if the electric is on."

"No, I'm gonna get it back on though." Then, the inspector asked to see a copy of her last bill.

"Yeah, hold on a minute," she said as she stormed back into the house. Then, like the idiot that she was, the tenant walked back out and handed the inspector the bill. Ike and the inspector's eyes both nearly popped out their heads. This moron owed $1,700! Don't ask me why her power wasn't cut off months ago, but it was not.

"Ma'am, how do you intend on paying this?"

"I'm gonna put the electric in my mom's name."

"No you're not!" the inspector snapped. "That's illegal. You can't run a bill up this high and then have someone else put it in their name."

"Well, that's the only way I can do it," was her reply.

What nerve some people have! It takes balls to just come out and tell you that the way they intend on paying the bill is by not paying it at all. Cheating or stealing would be another name for it. Anyway, the inspector told the tenant that her Service Rep would be notified and that if the electric bill wasn't paid in 72 hours, she would risk being thrown off the program. Now, Ike was on cloud nine as he danced off the front porch!

As soon as he got back to his office, he called his tenant and offered her a once in a lifetime deal. Here is what he told her. "I want you out of my house. Call your Service Rep and ask for an "emergency packet.' (An emergency packet enables the tenant to move immediately.) I don't care if you tell her I'm harassing you, I stole your meter, whatever, just get out! If you don't, here is what I'm gonna do for ya. Not only am I going to drag you back into court, I'm going to personally go down to the electric company and notify them on how you intend on beating them on the bill. I'm gonna make sure they are on the lookout for anyone trying to switch the electric for this property into their name. Then I'm going to your Service Rep with the electric bill and gas bill that you didn't pay and I'm going to put pressure on her to throw you off the system for not paying your utilities. If your Service Rep doesn't want to cooperate, I'll go to her boss. So, unless you've got 1,700 bucks laying around, I suggest you get the hell out of my house or you'll be paying rent for the rest of your life!" To Ike's delight, she was gone in eleven days.

Playing Dirty – Part II

Ike and Rick had a tenant who ran up a $512 water bill. They showed up at the tenant's house with bill in hand. "Mrs. Jones, you owe us $464 for your over usage of the water."

"What! I ain't paying that, your toilet is leaking!"

Sure enough, Ike went upstairs into the bathroom and the flapper valve was hung up. Water was just running and running. The tenant never even bothered to call Ike or Rick. When Ike showed her the two items in her lease that she signed stating that she was responsible for over usage and notifying the landlord about any leaks, she just shrugged it off and said there was no way she could come up with that kind of money. She didn't want to work out payment arrangements or anything. Simply put, up your ass landlord, I'm not paying it, is what she thought.

Well, Ike and Rick had a decision to make. Do they pay court costs and attorneys to drag this loser into court? For what? She is already telling them she's never going to pay. No, instead they came up with a better idea.

Ike went back to the office and called the water department. He told them he was installing a new main ball valve and needed the water shut off for a couple of days while he was doing the work. Since Ike and Rick keep the water bills in their name, they had no problem getting it shut off the very next day. The water was shut off at 9:00 a.m. The tenant was calling the office by 9:15 a.m. Rick answered the phone.

Rick said, "Hello."

Tenant said, "Hello Rick, this is Mrs. Jones. I don't have any water on over here."

"Yeah, that's too bad. We didn't have $464 either so we had the water company shut it off. We had a business decision to make, either pay our mortgage or pay your water bill and we chose the mortgage."

"You can't do that. I'm calling my Service Rep."

"Go right ahead. I'll be sitting here waiting to speak to her." Sure enough, within five minutes the phone is ringing again. Guess who? You got it, the tenant's Service Rep.

"Mr. Rick, I just got a call from an irate tenant of yours."

"Yeah, I know. She's no more irate than what I was yesterday when I received a $512 water bill that could have been prevented."

"Well, whatever the case, you have got to get that water turned back on."

Rick replied, "I don't think that is gonna happen."

"And why is that?"

"Because I don't have $512 bucks to get it back on."

Service Rep snapped, "Aahh, you're just being smart now."

"Whoa, whoa, whoa, wait a minute here. You don't even know the story. First of all, the tenant knew exactly what the leak was and never called us. Second of all, how come it's all right for the tenant not to have $500 bucks but it's not all right for me not to have $500 bucks? After paying a $400 mortgage on the joint and a $500 water bill to boot, I'd be losing $200 just to have this asshole stay in my property this month! I told her the same thing I'm telling you. I didn't use the water and I'm not paying for it. I'm paying my mortgage, not her water bill."

Well, after about two days of not showering, not flushing the toilet, and not brushing their teeth, I guess the tenant came to her senses. By some "miracle," she found a way to come up with the $464 bucks she owed!

Playing Dirty – Part III

Ike and Rick had a tenant for five years. Every year, the annual inspection repair list would get longer and longer. They would do the repairs, then hold their breath until the next year, hoping the repairs would lessen. One thing that they noticed is that every time they went to the property, it seemed more and more people were living there.

After walking through the property with the inspector on the annual inspection, Ike had had enough. Not only was the inspector pointing things out that needed repair, but the tenant also wanted to get involved! That's right, she started leading the inspector into areas of the home to show him what was broken. Some of these people have brass balls!

"I can see why shit in here is getting broken. You've got about 12 people shacking up in here!" Ike snapped at the tenant. "What the hell is this--a flop house?"

"They're not staying here; they're just visiting," the tenant said. "Yeah, well I didn't give them permission to visit and you're lying because they are the same bums who were sleeping on the floor last year. Try reading your lease under the part that says, 'No Visitors.'"

Panic immediately set in on the tenant's face and she didn't point out another thing for repair. "I'll have them out of here today, Mr. Ike."

About three days after the inspection, Ike received the repair list in the mail. He already knew it was going to be bad, but this thing was longer than the Constitution! He talked with Rick and it was time to fish or cut bait. Do the repairs or unload this steady homewrecker. They chose to get rid of the tenant.

Ike took the repair list over to the tenant's house to give her a copy and inform her that they wouldn't be doing any of the repairs. They would rather unload her, remodel the house, and rent it to someone who wanted to take care of the property. As Ike pulled up in his truck, the same bums that were sleeping on the floor three days ago were now out on the front steps partying down! Keep in mind it was only 10:30 in the morning. As Ike weaved through the partiers to get to the door, he told them they can't be hanging out front. Instead of leaving, they all started walking up the steps as if they were gonna go back in the house! "Yo, you can't hang in here either. You're not on the lease so take a hike." They left, but you know damn well that as soon as Ike drove away, they returned.

Anyway, as soon as Ike showed the tenant the repair list and informed her that she had to move because he wasn't going to do the repairs, she went nuts, yelling and screaming so loud that half the people on the block came out of their homes to see what was going on. Their loud, obnoxious yelling didn't intimidate Ike (or me and Nick), whatsoever. If you own the house, it's your choice on who you want to live there. All the yelling in the world will never change that!

Ike knew that if he didn't do the repairs and were to start an eviction, he would lose about three months' rent. He and Rick came up with another plan. First, they went down to Section 8 and had a talk with the fellow that was in charge of "Investigations." They told him that there were about 12 people living in the property. They asked him to do a little investigating and get back to them.

After only one day, the investigator called back. The investigator checked with the Postal Service and nine people were receiving mail at the property. Not only that, the electric, phone, and gas were all in other people's names that weren't even on the lease!

Ike couldn't wait to call the tenant and tell her what he had found out. You could hear a pin drop while he ran down the list of the names each utility was in. Once again, that offer that Ike loves so much was put on the table. "Get the hell out of my house or lose your voucher due to utility fraud!" She was gone in two weeks.

Final Thought on Playing Dirty

When you decide to play dirty, sometimes the ball bounces your way. The first thing you've got to do is get the ball in play. If you sit idly on the sidelines, you'll never know which way the ball might have bounced. Whether it would have gone your way or the tenant's way, you'll never know if you don't take some type of action.

Another thing I've learned about playing dirty is that even if it doesn't work out quite the way you wanted it to, it puts the tenants back on their heels a little bit. Rather than thinking about which way they're going to screw with you, they become more worried about what you're going to do to them! I know you may not believe this but, I truly believe they respect you a little more. Either that or they think you're nuts, which isn't bad because fear is also a form of respect.

Every tenant in the world who goes to court, lies and wins, would love for their landlord to hang his head in defeat.

"I ain't that landlord!" You see, I also know they lied and when your tenant lies in court, they open up the doors to a dirty playing field. After you begin to turn the tables on them, they now go on the defensive. You're making life just as miserable for them as they have been making it for you. A saying that I love to use is, "if I get the tenant from hell, I become the landlord from hell." That's when the false promises start coming in. The ones like, "If one more thing goes wrong around here or one more thing disappears, I'm taking you to court." Guess what, you've already been there so that shouldn't deter you in the slightest. What's the court gonna do, put you in jail because the lady who owes a $1,700 electric bill is missing an electric meter?

Here's the kicker! Once you've turned the tables, the tenant has to now take you to court. That would involve picking up the phone and finding out how to get to landlord/tenant court, taking about three trolley rides and two subways to get there, coming up with the money to get the case started, and killing another half a day, standing in lines. That would be too much like work and judging by my experience, I'm about 95% sure that won't happen. She would just as soon leave!!!

Look, I know that playing dirty is not for everyone. You either have it in you or you don't. Who knows, maybe I am a cold-hearted son of a bitch but when somebody is trying to take or destroy something that belongs to me, I'm gonna fight. If they lie, I'm gonna lie; if they cheat, I'm gonna cheat. In order to preserve your self-respect, it is sometimes necessary to lie and cheat!

You pretty much know that you've got a lowlife for a tenant when it gets as far as the courtroom, so who cares what they think of you. It's your house, your time, and your money that you stand to lose, so why not try to get them out of your property before it gets to the courtroom? You shouldn't feel one bit guilty about playing dirty. Hopefully, your tenant will get tired of your mischievous ways and try their luck with another landlord. What have you got to lose … a bad tenant?

CHAPTER 3

KNOWING THE RULE BOOK

Every Section 8 office has a rulebook. Most are pretty similar, pretty straight forward, and always change! To stay ahead you've got to be on top of the rulebook. Know what the rules are and when the rule changes go into effect and you should be alright. It's the things that some inspectors pull out of the thin air that get me totally aggravated. Here's what I'm talking about.

We had a house that was passing inspection with flying colors until the inspector walked out back. Here is how the conversation went:

Inspector said, "Everything in the house is fine but I have to fail you for these steps."

"What the hell is wrong with the steps?"

These were the three steps that I fought the insepctor and won on. I see that since we sold the property, the inspector must have finally gotten his way. Notice there is now a railing on 28 inch steps!

Inspector replied, "You need a railing here because there are three steps."

"But they're not over 30 inches." (I knew they weren't because we measured them when we wrote our list.)"Are you sure?"

Me, "Positive."

"Well it's a judgment call and I'm going to say you need a railing here."

"What the f*ck are you talking about a judgment call? Your ass is a judgment call, but my steps are not a judgment call! They're 28 inches and your rulebook calls for anything over 30 inches high to have a railing. You wrote the damn thing, not me.I If I didn't tell you what the rulebook called for, I'd bet my life you wouldn't know what the requirements were."

"Look, I'm gonna cut you a break this time but next time you've got to have a railing here."

I said, "You're not cutting me any break and I'll never put a railing on steps that don't exceed 30 inches. You would be cutting me a break if my steps were 31 inches but they're not. I know what your rulebook says and I follow it to a tee, so don't invent 'judgment calls.'"

Needless to say, I passed and never did that inspector ever try to fail me again for a railing violation. Hell, after giving him an earful, I probably could have had 35-inch steps with no railing and gotten away with it! Point is, if the inspector knows you know the rulebook like the back of your hand, he'll be less likely to question you on it. I have literally bullshitted a couple of inspectors that the railing requirements were 36 inches and have gotten away with it. You would think that they would know the requirements but most of them don't and don't care.

Even the ballbreakers will put on a show and tell you what you need, but if you question or challenge them on something that you know is right, they'll back up. Don't be afraid or intimidated by these guys. Argue with them because they are not always right. Some people have so much respect for their superiors that they have none left for themselves. Remember, these inspectors are not your superiors or your boss. They simply come out to inspect the house that you own. You won't be fired or suspended from the program if your house doesn't pass an inspection, so speak up and give them hell!

Inspectors really don't have to know the rulebook because at the end of the week they will still be getting their paychecks. You need to know the rulebook because you may be failing inspections that you should be passing! Without passing inspections, you won't be getting a paycheck.

Think about the scenario I just gave you. If I would have let the inspector fail me for a "judgment call," I would have been out some serious cash. It would have cost me about $200 bucks to get a wrought iron railing made up and at least two weeks to have the railing made up and mounted. That's another half month's rent at about $400 bucks. I would have lost a total of $600 bucks for nothing...something I was already in good shape on. Don't let it happen to you either. The rulebook is the only thing you need to memorize in this business, and you can read it in a weekend's time. If knowledge (or inspectors) can create problems, it is not through ignorance that we can solve them. The price one pays for pursuing any profession is an intimate knowledge of its ugly side (Baldwin).

I cannot stress to you enough how important and handy this book can be to you! Everything you need to know is in here. It helps you eliminate, lets you know what you need in your unit to pass inspection, and what you cannot have in the unit if you intend to pass your inspection. It also gives you ammo – ammo in the form of proof. Although an inspector may not like the way you made a repair or eliminated a certain item, as long as it's in the rulebook or not in the rulebook, he cannot fail you. A lot of times it's a gray area and I'll walk a fine line between what the rulebook says and what the inspector says. But, hey, as long as I'm going by what their rulebook says, then I'm playing by the rules!

I really don't care how ridiculous a certain repair may look or how strange an inspector finds it that you eliminated a certain item. As long as it saves you time, money, and you can validate your actions using 'their rulebook,' you'll be in good shape. If I continue to save cash by eliminating things that I don't need, I'll play these games until the cows come home!

I told you in Volume I how we will cover up a hole in the ceiling with a piece of luan and paint it white. Well, I had an inspector challenge me on it because "he didn't like the way it looked." My response to him as I handed him the rulebook was, "Show me where it says you can't patch a hole in the ceiling with luan." He couldn't and I passed the inspection. I'm not out here for a beauty contest; I'm out here to make cash. He is not an interior decorator, he's an inspector and if I have to remind him of that fact, I will.

I also had an inspector challenge me on our removal of washing machine hookups. This one was an easy winner! I simply handed him the rulebook and said, "Find me the chapter that even mentions 'washing machines or washing machine hookups.'" He didn't even bother looking at the rulebook and just passed back to me. At least the other inspector paged through the book, looking to see what a hole could be patched with. If it doesn't say it in black and white that I have to give them a washer hookup, they ain't getting one, period!

The point is when you know your shit, it can save your thousands of dollars. You can get more and more creative and you'll have a leg (the rulebook) to stand on if you are challenged.

It won't take you long to learn the rulebook and soon you will know it like the back of your hand. In other professions you might have to read fifty or sixty books to become an expert on a certain subject. With Section 8 Housing, it's only one book, so don't be lazy. Get busy reading the only book (other than mine!) that you will need in this field, the rulebook!

Here is another tip. Get a pen and some paper out while reading the rulebook. Write down some things you can eliminate, some shortcuts you can take, and anything else that will be helpful to you while getting your unit ready for inspection. Oh yeah, and one more thing. ALWAYS bring the rulebook with you to your inspections! It's worth its weight in gold when an inspector wants to fail you on something that he may think is wrong and you have the rules in your back pocket that you know are correct. Knowledge is power; use it wisely and to your advantage!

CHAPTER 4

DUPLEXES AND MULTIFAMILY UNITS

The question, "Are you guys for or against multi-family units?" came up a lot. I'll cut right to the chase. When renting to Section 8 tenants, I don't get involved with them and I'll tell you a couple of reasons why.

I'm not a big fan of duplexes.

#1. Responsibility or lack of it. That is exactly what you get. We owned a triplex which consisted of three two-bedroom units. The basement which contained the utilities (heater, hot water heater) was off limits to the tenants. It had a separate entrance with a keyed lock. The tenants were to have no access to the basement at all. (You see where this story is going, don't ya!)

Well, about ten months had passed and it was time for our Section 8 annual inspection. A couple of minor repairs were needed in one of the units and the other two passed inspection. When I went outside with the inspector to open the basement door, my key wouldn't work. The Qwikset key that I had in my hand with the "B" written on it for 'basement' was the correct key, but the lock was now replaced with a Titan deadbolt lock. I lost it!I ran up the steps and started banging on all three tenant's doors like Fred Flintstone. Nobody knew anything and it was like honor amongst thieves. "Okay, if that's the way we're gonna play it, fine. I'm gonna rip the lock off and if I find one shred of mail, one piece of trash, one piece of anything with any of your names on it, I'm going to have the inspector (who was standing right beside me enjoying the show) write it up. Then me and him are gonna march it back down to your Service Rep and terminate your ass." I felt like a fifth-grade teacher trying to find out who put the tack on my seat. Anyway, as I walked towards my truck to get my tools, one of them spoke up.

"Mr. Mike, if I get you the key, are you still gonna evict me?" "Probably," I shot back. "It depends on what the basement looks like... now go get the key." She ran upstairs and returned with the key. "My uncle got laid off from work and he's just been sleeping down here for a couple of months," she said.

When I opened the door, I couldn't believe my eyes. Our triplex had been turned into a quadplex without us even knowing about it! It was like what Arsenio Hall did to Eddie Murphy's apartment in "Coming to America." This guy had a leather couch, coffee table, 50" television and a mattress all jammed onto a 12 ft. × 12 ft. leopard skin rug! And, oh yeah, pictures hanging on Structolite cement walls. It was like putting earrings on a pig. The tenant stood there silent, waiting to see how I was going to react. I stood there shocked. The inspector looked at me and said, "Living large!" Well, with that, we both fell out of the basement in hysterics!

As for the tenant, I told her she had to have the basement cleared out by 4:00 p.m. and that she also needed to come up with $40 bucks for the lock that I would be replacing on the basement door. She did both and I leaped over my first hurdle.

About a month or so later, I get three, not one, calls that all my tenant's sinks and toilets are backed up. By the time I get there, the Section 8 inspector is already there. As I pull up the driveway, I see one of my tenants standing out there talking to him. I get out of my truck and start walking toward them. Of course, it's the sneak that had her uncle holed up in my basement.

"Hi Mr. Mike, did you get my message?"

Of course I got it...did she think I was just dropping by to say hello? "Yeah, I got it. You only left it about an hour ago."

" I couldn't get a hold of you so I called Section 8 this morning."

I know the game; I've been around a long time and when your tenant calls Section 8 on you, it's personal. It's for no other reason than to get you in a bind with Section 8 and to jeopardize your monthly payment. I know that, she knows that, and the inspector knows that. Yet we all have to stand around like three jerkoffs and pretend like we don't.

Believe me, I can understand if a tenant is having a problem that they had nothing to do with, such as a roof leaking, no heat, etc. and they call the landlord again and again and get no response. They have every right to complain then but, come on, one hour? I'm not a slumlord and if there is a problem I'm responsible for, I'm going to fix it. That's just part of the business but at least give me time to get into the office and check the messages.

I already knew the inspector was going to give me a '24-hour violation' and that was fine. (A 24-hour violation means you have one day to fix the problem.) The main drain was clogged. We sent our plumber over to run the snake through the line and the problem was cleared up in about an hour.

No problem you would think, right? You send a plumber over, pay him $80 bucks, and your property is good as new and ready to pass inspection. That's how the foolish mind thinks; mine goes deeper. All day long and half of the night, I thought about how that seemingly innocent event could have turned out much worse.

What if we didn't get the line open? What if the curb trap was broken at the street? Well, you would have to pull a permit down at City Hall to have the street dug up. That could take about a week. God forbid it happens on a Thursday or Friday because you're going to lose Saturday and Sunday because City Hall is closed. Meanwhile, you have got three different families whose waste is going down one clogged pipe. You're soon going to be up to your knees in you know what! That's your first worry.

Here is your second. The Section 8 inspector gave you one day to clear the line. The next day he returns, the line is not cleared and you failed the re-inspection. Now let's suppose all three units were rented each for $700 per month. That would give you $2,100 per month in rent. Break that down into days and you're looking at $70 buck a day ($2,100 divided by 30 days = $70). After the Section 8 inspector fails you, you will not be getting paid on any of these three units. Let's say it takes eight days to get the work done, schedule another inspection, and get the property back on the payroll. You just lost $560 in rent, not to mention what you're going to pay for the plumber and the city permit. Had it been only a single family unit, you would have lost only $186 in rent!

Fortunately, during the short time we owned the triplex, that nightmare never played itself out. Unfortunately, another one did. Once again, I received three, not one, calls about no heat. Of course, it had to be the day after Christmas and about 5 degrees, not to mention that every tenant had every single relative and their brother over the house. I was tempted to throw the leopard skin rug down and hang the pictures back up in the basement. Maybe I could rent it out to one of them for $50 a night as a one-bedroom flat!

Nick and I couldn't get the heater fired up, so we called our heater guy out. "Bad news guys, it's beat and everybody is closed until Monday." Well, everyone but Section 8, that is. After feeling like the

Grinch who stole Christmas and informing all three families that there won't be any heat until Monday…you got it! All three families called Section 8 on us. I can't say I blame them and I felt bad myself (sort of), but there was nothing Nick or I could do. It was just bad timing and shit luck, I guess.

Of course, the relatives wanted to get loud and start a commotion. "Well, what are you gonna do, go back to your nice warm house and leave us out in the cold?"

(Why yes, that's exactly what I was going to do now that the guy mentioned it). First of all, this was a guy who was visiting and we didn't owe him any explanation at all but, ya know, you try to be civilized. "Buddy, look," I tried to explain.

"I ain't your buddy," he snapped.

"No shit, but you were yesterday when your ass was up in my house with the heat on!" I shot back.

"This ain't about heat…it's about me coming up here from Florida to visit and everything getting ruined!" That's when Nick jumped in his face.

"Yeah jackass, your visit to our house got ruined when our heater died. We're not too happy about paying two grand to replace it either. What vital part do you play in this? You don't live here, and you don't have to come up with the cash to replace the damn thing…so what's your bitch?" (Quote: He that blows the coals in quarrels that he has nothing to do with has no right to complain if the sparks fly in his face.) Still, the visitor wanted to keep it going.

"I came all the way up from Florida to visit, not freeze." That's when Nick hit him with one of his famous one-liners.

"Yeah, well you should have stayed down there where it's warm."

Needless to say, we lost about six days rent totaling $420 bucks! Had it been a single-family unit, we would have only lost $139.

Weekend -boxing matches at the triplex! Here is another thing you'll get when you own multi-family units…fist fights and rumbles. We owned our triplex for fourteen months. The police were out there eleven times for altercations! One week the tenant in B is fighting with the tenant in C; the next week they're both fighting with the tenant in A. It's weird when you go over there to raise hell about something they broke or destroyed, and they stick together like a pack of rats and blame you. The minute you leave, they go back to killing each other. I can't figure it out!

One summer weekend I was in the office on a Saturday afternoon. The tenant from Apt. A had called to inform me that there was a full-blown battle going on in the backyard of the property. She told me that what started out as a barbeque had now turned into World War III. She said that there were about thirty people going at it! From what I could hear from the noise coming through the phone, I would have guessed 130 people were going at it.

"What do you want me to do? Call the damn cops," I yelled!

"Well, you're the landlord; come break this thing up," she said.

Yeah, right, I could just see my lily-white ass walking into the yard and yelling, "Hey everybody, stop fighting. I'm the landlord!" They would have stopped all right…just for the amount of time it would have taken to beat me into submission. Then it would have been back to the free for all. God forbid, if the guy that Nick told to stay in Florida was up 'visiting' again. I would have certainly been killed.

The point I am trying to make here is that when you've got three tenants living on top of each other, it's like they're living in a powder keg and each tenant is giving off sparks. Whether it's about noise, parking, leaks, garbage, girlfriends, boyfriends, etc., something is going to happen…mark my words. And when it does, it won't settle down. It'll be like the Hatfields and McCoys. Soon, Section 8 and the police will want you to be the sheriff. You can pin that badge on somebody else!

Let's go over the pros and cons of multi-family units. Cons first.

#1. There is no accountability. You can't hold one specific person or unit responsible for anything. If the main drain gets clogged, you had three families flushing their toilets into it so you can't pin the clog on any of them. No one will own up to it and all you'll get is finger pointing and blaming which will lead to fisticuffs and arrests.

#2. Problems to the third power! If one thing goes wrong, you've got three people calling you. Worse yet, you've got three people calling Section 8. When you come over to check out a problem, you've got three tenants flocking to you to tell you about ten other problems that they are having. Eye-yie-yie, you'll never get back home.

#3. Loss of rent! If Section 8 has to stop your pay for any type of utility or backup problem, you're now losing rent on three units at a time.

#4. Fires! God forbid there is a fire. You might lose three of your investments in one day! I could go on with the cons all day, but I'm sure by now you get the point.

Now, let me give the pros.

#1. Tax! You're only paying taxes on one unit instead of three (triplex) or four (quad).

#2. Insurance. You're only paying to insure one unit instead of three or four. You don't have to insure each unit separately, just the building.

My answer to both of these pros is, "big deal." The cons heavily outweigh the pros.

One more thing about multi-family units and how nice guys finish last. One of my tenants that lived in the triplex was a terrific tenant as well as a very hardworking lady. She worked in a deli where I would grab lunch about once a week. It didn't matter what time or what day I was in there, she would be working regardless. She lived in the apartment with her mother and son, worked about fifty hours a week, kept an immaculate apartment, and was always on time with her portion of the rent. One specific day, I walked into the store and she asked if she could speak to me for a minute. "The man that owns the store is closing this one and opening up in a different location in three weeks. Could I hold back on this month's rent and I will double up on next month's?" I knew the woman to be a very hard worker and was positive she wasn't out to play games. The next month, just as she said, I was paid in full. If that's how this story ended, I wouldn't be telling it!

Not even a week later, I get a call from the woman downstairs who is now a week late on her rent. "Mike, can I speak with you a minute?"

Uh oh, this is starting to sound all too familiar. "Yeah, go ahead" I said. "I was wondering if you could let me slide my rent on until next month and I'll pay everything up."

"No, you can't," I answered. "Why not?"

"Because your rent portion is only $70 bucks and I don't need you getting behind, that's why." Keep in mind that this was the same woman whose uncle was squatting in my basement and the same woman who loves calling Section 8 on me the minute a floorboard creaks.

"You mean you can let Mrs. Natasha slide a month but you can't let me? I have problems too!" One time, one time I feel like having a heart and again it bites me in the ass! The woman who worked in the deli could have given Nick free hoagies and sodas for a year and he still wouldn't have let her go on the rent. I do her a favor and she tells the entire complex! I couldn't go up to her apartment and blast her because, hey, she might have just been telling the story of what happened and saying that I'm a nice guy. Well, the low life downstairs heard 'nice guy' and, like a shark, must have smelled blood in the water. 'Nice guy' sounds more like 'sucker' to her so I guess she thought she'd try her luck.

"Why can't you come up with $70 bucks?" I asked.

"Because my son's father usually pays it and he is out of the state until next month."

"Oh, yeah, does Section 8 know he pays your portion of the rent?"

"No," she said.

"Well, let me put it to you cut and dry. I know Natasha and I know what she's about. That's why I cut her a break. I don't know your son's father and I'm not gonna wait for him to pay rent that he doesn't owe me. You owe me $70 bucks. Pay it or I'll start the eviction today."

"Fine, I'll pay it, but I'm moving the f*** out of here. You play favorites!"

Man, I wish I had a buck for every tenant that didn't get their way and told me they were moving out. We sold the triplex about eight years ago, with her still in it, and I'll bet she still calls the place home. Wouldn't doubt that the uncle tried his luck at moving back into the basement either!

Anyway, another con with multi-family units is that if you do a repair or cut someone a break, they'll all expect one or think that they have one coming. Stick to the single family units…they're less headaches. And, oh yeah, don't cut any breaks. Believe me, if you're a nice guy in this profession, you'll not only finish last, you'll also finish broke!

CHAPTER 5

ELIMINATION

Elimination, always a favorite topic of mine! I could talk about elimination all day and never get bored with it. Stick me in a room with a couple of landlords who know a little bit about elimination and I'll think I died and went to heaven. So imagine the joy I've been in since releasing the Section 8 Bible Volume I.

Every day, landlords send me over an e-mail with an item that they have eliminated along with a juicy story of why they eliminated it. When I get feedback from some of you who told me they were not eliminating anything and after reading Volume I, they have now seen the light, I get goose bumps. When they tell me how much cash they started saving after elimination, well, I can't tell you what else I get because you'd really think I'm sick!

I would have sworn there wasn't anything left that you could eliminate from a house that we didn't know of. I must admit, we were wrong. Nick and I found a couple more things on our own and some other landlords came up with a couple of winners…so here we go!

Antennas – Antennas are something that we have always eliminated but forgot to tell you in Volume I. Yes, even we make mistakes. Before the roofer coats your roof or puts down a rubber roof, have him remove the antenna if there is still one on the roof. Not only do some of these things look like they're trying to reach Mars, but they also sit on a 12" × 12" base that is either screwed or bolted into the roof. If your roofer is installing all new rubber, why have him skip or go around the 1' × 1' section under the antenna? Everybody has cable these days and the antenna is pretty much obsolete.

Remove your antenna before installing a rubber roof.

Another thing that can and has happened is if there are strong winds, the antenna can pull away from the roof. One of its many pointed poles can now puncture your new rubber roof. If you're giving your roofer the job of putting on a new roof, he probably won't even charge you to remove the antenna.

Slag roofs – We told you in Volume I that if you have a slag roof, wait for it to leak, then just replace the entire roof with rubber instead of trying to repair it. Well, still replace the roof with rubber…just don't wait for it to leak. Do it immediately when you purchase the property! If you own any properties with slag roofs replace them now. Why the change of heart? Here is why.

We told you a slag roof is millions of tiny stones laid evenly across the roof. It has become an outdated way of roofing, replaced by tar and rubber roofs. So if you have a slag roof, it is old, real old. However, that's not my reason for concern. This is. Over the last two years after we released Volume I, we have seen two roofs that were slag which collapsed! That's right, they totally caved in. And do you know why they caved in? Not because they were old, but because of lazy, jerked off roofers!

Ya see, instead of removing the stones the correct way before installing the new rubber roof, which would be using a chute and dumpster to haul away the stones, they used a wheelbarrow.

Roofers moved stone from roof to roof with a wheel barrell.

That's right! They would find another unsuspecting homeowner on that side of the street that also had a slag roof and simply just dump the stones on their roof. Now, the homeowner does not even know that he has twice as much stone on top of his head than he had the previous day. Finally, when another lazy roofer decided to come along and dump his stone on the same rooftop for load number three, the roof couldn't hold it anymore. Thank God, nobody was home when a couple tons of stone came crashing through the house!

I've actually seen some slag roofs that look like they had the amount of four or five roofs on them. You're going to be replacing your slag roof anyway so why not do it now and get it out of the way before it leads to a serious problem.

Radiator covers -
don't need'em!

Radiator covers – Well, you can thank a royal pain in the ass of an inspector for this one. For years, this guy broke 'em for us about radiator covers. "You need a radiator cover in the bedroom," or "the radiator cover is cracked," or "the radiator cover's paint is chipping." I would have sworn this guy owned a radiator cover company.

Finally, we had a small radiator in a bathroom that only had three heating fins on it. Not only did it have just three fins but it sat inside the bathroom closet. Wouldn't you know this guy found it and insisted we needed a cover! He told me to get a cover on it, call him back, and he would come back out and complete the initial inspection.

This time, unlike the previous fifty times, instead of making up a radiator cover, I grabbed the rulebook. I searched high and low and found nothing saying we needed a radiator cover. There was a small section that would help me with my argument. In this section it simply said that all existing radiators must be operable and that at least one was needed in each room. Also, and here is where it gets good, all radiators that do not have a cover must be free of chipping or peeling paint. My interpretation was, "Hello radiators, goodbye radiator covers!

I called the inspector and told him I would be ready for him the next day. I couldn't stop smiling all over myself, knowing that I had out- maneuvered him. Here's the bitch. Even though you know you're right and the rulebook agrees with you, you know you're going to get some half-assed argument out of these guys so just be prepared. It can be written in black and white and be as plain as the nose on their face, but for some reason, they still want to argue sometimes. I swear to you that if I was an inspector and someone told me you don't need a front door, I'd be like, "Where does it say that?" If they showed it to me in the rulebook, I'd say, "Okay, you passed. Do you wanna hang a curtain or some beads across the front there so the flies don't get in?"

Anyway, the next day, I was at the property and up pulled 'Mr. Check It.' Up the steps he went, headed directly for the bathroom closet. I waited downstairs in fear I would laugh in his face. "Aren't you forgetting something up here?"

"Nah, Tom, I checked the rulebook and you don't need radiator covers to pass inspection."

"Sure, you do," he answered as he walked down the steps. "I've been making you install them for years."

"Yeah, but that doesn't mean I need them or it doesn't make it right. The only thing you've had me doing for years is wasting time and money."

"Sorry, Mike, I can't let you go on a safety issue."

"Tom, you're not letting me go, the rulebook is. And safety? Why would a radiator in a closet be any safer with or without a radiator cover?"

"Somebody can fall and crack their head on that radiator, that's why."

"Yeah, right, in a closet!" I snapped back.

"I'm not going to argue with you, Mike," he said as he threw up his hands.

"I know, and neither am I. I brought the rulebook with me so we wouldn't have any arguments. Take a look at it and show me where it says 'all radiators must have covers.'" Of course, he couldn't find anything and he hit me with the infamous, 'I'm going to cut you a break' line. I guess when they know you've got them, they want to act like they're doing you a favor and save face.

Don't let them act like they are doing you a favor! Why, you ask? Because, the next time they'll want to hold 'that favor' against you. It'll go something like this. "Last week I cut you a break with that radiator cover but I can't do it this time." You don't have to be spiteful or a smartass but let them know.

Here is a good way to answer it so it rules out anything in the future. "Tom, you're really not cutting me a break because I don't, nor ever did, I need radiator covers." Don't worry about hurting his feelings and don't thank him for 'cutting you a break' for something you didn't need a break on. You were already in the right. Only a coward or a fool apologizes for being right.

Also, one more thing about radiator covers. Did you know they actually engineered a test and found that 99% of tenant's heads are harder than the radiator itself? Nick and I applied for the job as testers for this study. You know, we wanted to be the guys who actually tested the tenant's head against the radiator.

Unfortunately, we were told that this position had already been filled by other landlords who volunteered for this position! We were also told that the line to fill out an application for this position was five miles long. If you or any other landlord that you know has participated in this study, please let us know about your experience!

Standing mailbox

Mailboxes – I know, , you need a mailbox to pass inspection. Even a tenant needs a place to receive their mail (example of tenant's mail: eviction notices, copy of water bill over usage notices, overdue rent notices, etc.). Just don't give them the wall mounted type!

Tenants will have this mailbox ripped from the wall in no time.

I don't know why, but half the time they don't even open them up to take their mail out. Meanwhile, the mailman keeps stuffing and stuffing away. Next thing you know, the mailbox pulls away from the wall and God knows what happens to it after that. If it doesn't come disconnected from the wall, it's a good bet the lid gets broken off from being overstuffed. Either way, a broken lid or a missing mailbox is a reason to fail inspection.

What's the answer? Simply cut a hole in the door and get the old fashion type of mailbox!

Door slot mailboxes are the best!

They can't overstuff it or rip the lid off. Do it once to your property and you're done forever. Also, your tenant will be forced to pick their mail up off the floor and open anything you have sent them.

Yard with many broken concrete blocks

Concrete yards – For years we have been taping together, patching, and replacing concrete blocks in our rental property's backyards. If the inspector finds a block that is cracked…. or not level…you've got to replace or fix it. A 4' × 4' block usually costs about $125 to replace. If the inspector tells you to replace five or six of them, well, you do the math. It can and did get very expensive.

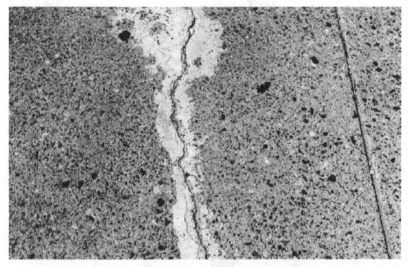

Cracked concrete blocks

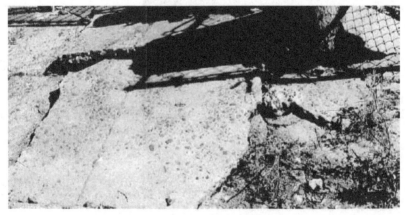

And unlevel concrete blocks!

Anyway, we had a yard that had ten blocks in it. Eight of the blocks needed to be replaced. We pulled up the stake body, got out the sledgehammers and went to town. That's when an idea went off in my head like a light bulb! 'Eliminate all ten blocks, even the two good ones. Then thrown down some grass seed and call it a day.'

The concrete yard...now became a grass yard and it saved me about $1,200. Grass seed is cheaper than concrete and, besides, you'll get a little exercise breaking up the concrete while saving a buck!

Concrete yard has now become a grass yard!

Okay, now I'll get to some of those landlord e-mails. I think this "elimination thing" is catching on. Not only is it catching on, it's also a lot of fun. The more fun you have and the more money you'll save! The best part is that you're eliminating things before the tenant moves in. By the time they get there, they had no idea that there was a dishwasher or a screen door on the property. They can ask for either one, but they won't be getting their wish. Now for those e-mails!

Email #1 from James Blanch, Haddonfield, New Jersey

"Mike and Nick, wonderful job! Me and my wife sat at the dinner table passing your book back and forth and laughed our asses off. My favorite chapter was that of elimination...loved it! I have been doing Section 8 land lording for quite a while and although I do eliminate several things, you guys have me beat by a long shot.

"One thing that I like to eliminate from my rentals is a stove exhaust fan.

*Landlord –
eliminates
exhaust fan
above stove.*

"It seemed every single time we went out to do an inspection at a certain property of mine, we failed the inspection because the fan wasn't working or the light bulb was blown out. When she finally moved out, I removed the exhaust fan once and for all. I didn't replace it with a new one. What I did was I purchased a stove tin...that goes above the stove exactly where I removed the exhaust fan from. It keeps the heat from the stove off the cabinets and it keeps me passing my inspections. There was a window in the kitchen so the exhaust fan was not needed for ventilation, therefore, making the exhaust fan useless.

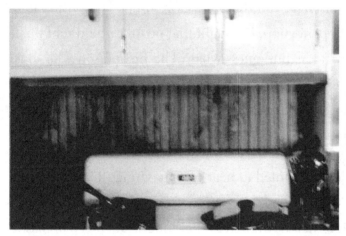

And replaces it with metal stove tin (fire shield).

"I am enclosing a picture of the stove tin in case you want to use it in your next book. If I think of anything else between now and the release of Volume II, I'll shoot you over another e-mail. Once again, great work guys!"

James, thanks for the e-mail and, you're right! A 'stove tin' as you call it is a lot cheaper than an exhaust fan and will certainly never need a new motor or a light bulb replaced. The only problem as you mentioned is ventilation. I checked, and in some rulebooks, your stove has to be within four feet of a window to be able to eliminate an exhaust fan. So, before you rip out the exhaust fan, measure your distance and check your rule books.

One thing that I would like to add is that if an inspector failed me on inspection for an exhaust fan light bulb being blown out, I think I would have had to stuff him in the oven!

Email #2 from David DeFelice, Little Rock, Arkansas

"Mike and Nick, your book was awesome! The 'carpet in a can' worked to perfection. I thought that no one would rent the house with gray floors but, guess what? The first person who looked at the property took it. Your book already saved me about $800 in carpet and I just received it last month. Now I'm going to return the favor.

"You said you wanted to hear of some things that other landlords eliminate, and I have a few. The first is toilet paper holders. Can you believe that down here if that little white piece of plastic that the toilet paper spins on is missing, you'll fail inspection! As soon as I finished your book, that became the number one item that I began pulling from my properties. Something, as little as that must have cost me about ten inspections. Now, I tell the tenant to sit the toilet paper on the back of the toilet.

"The second thing that I began eliminating was the towel bars in the bathrooms. If the inspector found a broken one, again he would fail me, so down they came also. I'm getting pretty good at elimination and you'll be hearing from me very soon on some more things that I find!"

Dave, I wouldn't say you totally returned the favor, eight hundred bucks vs. what does a towel bar cost…twelve, thirteen bucks? I'd say I'm still in the lead and you still owe me! How about purchasing twenty books and, we'll call it even.

Just kidding Dave, I'm glad I've got you in the eliminating frame of mind. I've never failed an inspection for something as petty as a toilet paper tube missing but, hey, if you're failing the inspections because of it, eliminate it. As far as the towel bars, maybe your tenant was using it to do his chin ups!

Email #3 from Scott McBreen, Providence, Rhode Island

"Mike, I received the book on Thursday and finished it over the weekend. I found another thing that you can add to the elimination chapter……cabinets! Not the cabinets themselves but the cabinet handles. We are continuously failing inspections due to missing cabinet handles. I don't have the slightest idea of how they come off or where they end up, but it was sending me up a wall."Now, whenever I put in a new kitchen, I get the handle-less cabinets. How they work is you have a groove cut out at the bottom of the cabinet where you can slide your fingers under and open the cabinet. No more knobs or handles are needed! I will never fail another inspection for cabinet handles again.

"You would have loved it! The inspector came into the kitchen and told me that I failed because none of the cabinets had handles on them. I slipped my fingers into the groove, flung open the door and said, 'I don't think so!'"

"Great book, great ideas, and I'm really looking forward to Volume II. Don't cheat us; make it every bit as good as your first work of art!!"

Scott, you had me scared there for a minute! I thought you were going to tell me to make the tenants keep their food at a neighbor's house! Yes, I have also failed a couple of inspections due to missing cabinet handles. I have also failed some inspections for missing cabinet doors if you can believe that. And, no, I'm not gonna cheat anyone! I'm going to make Volume II every bit as good if not better than Volume I.

Let me end this chapter by saying this famous quote. "We often give our enemies the means of our own destruction." Sure this quote was made in war time but aren't you at war right now? Are you fighting to keep your money in your pocket where it belongs? Are you fighting to not waste another second of your time fixing things that you don't need to fix? Are you constantly fighting with tenants who break things and inspectors that tell you to fix these things? Then, my friends, you are at war!

Lucky for you, I know how to win the war and make the enemy surrender. Give them nothing to break and the inspectors won't break your balls. Give them nothing extra and they won't ask for anything extra. It's all about discipline and discipline is not a bad thing. Discipline is not something you do to someone, it's something you do for someone and that someone is not your tenant...it's yourself.

CHAPTER 6

STORIES – STORIES – STORIES

Stories! By far and away this was the number one feedback topic. So many of you landlords loved hearing about the stories that Nick and I told. I don't know if you liked the stories more than the learning but if I were to judge by the e-mails, I would say you liked the stories better!

I got to thinking why and I may have figured it out. It's almost like misery loves company. I think every landlord that has spent time in the trenches can tell you a funny, or scary, or crazy story about their experiences. The more homes you own, the more tenants you have and the more stories you have to tell.

When you read it coming from another landlord, you can relate and laugh about it. Maybe a woman running a Laundromat in her basement or someone filling a pool isn't a cause to go ballistic. Believe me, when I tell the story of it happening to me, I still get pissed! Yet, when I receive an e-mail about what happened to another landlord, I laugh hysterically! I guess it is human nature. Life is tough and, if you have the ability to laugh at it, you have the ability to enjoy it. I often use humor when trying to get a point across. Why? Because humor is like a rubber sword…it allows you to make a point without drawing blood.

Bad luck has to end up on someone and, when you're in this business, you just hope it's not you. Don't get me wrong. I laugh even harder if the landlord comes up with a scheme to outwit the tenant in the end.What I'm trying to say here is I love stories as much as the next guy! In this chapter, I am going to tell you a couple of mine and Nick's. Also, I'm gonna include a couple of good ones from some landlords who e-mailed in. So here we go!

Story #1 – It couldn't have been more than three weeks since I completed Volume I and bragged to you that I never had to pull my gun. Well, that's what I get for bragging!

It was a cold Friday, February night. I was up in the office until about 11:30 p.m. and I was getting ready to get out of there and head to my truck which was about a block away. As I always did before leaving the office at night, I took my 38 revolver out of the holster and slipped it into my jacket pocket with my hand on the grip. I pulled the office door shut and I was on my way.

I had to walk to the top of the street and hang a left at the corner. As I approached the corner, I heard them. I hadn't turned the corner yet but, by the sounds of it, it sounded like there were ten of them. I turned the corner and there they were five of them about thirty yards up and approaching quickly. When they saw me, dead silence! Common sense told me to cross the street. Two began to follow.

Street smarts told me to start crossing back and, if they followed, they were looking for trouble.

Sure enough, they started crossing back with me! My hand was already on the gun. I cocked back the hammer as hard as I could, hoping and knowing they would hear it. It made a sound that you or I wouldn't recognize, but they did. You and I know the sound of a screw gun spinning, a circular saw cutting, or Windows firing up on your computer. They happen to know the sound of a hammer of a gun getting cocked back and ready to fire.

They both stopped dead in their tracks!

"Somebody's gonna get hurt out here" I said.

"Sir, we were just gonna ask you for a cigarette."

"I don't smoke so get the f_ _ _ on the other side of the street," I said as I continued walking briskly.

They didn't say another word, nor did they follow me. Even though I was loaded for bear, it's still a very scary situation that I hope I'm never put in again. The only gun I will ever carry is a revolver. Believe me, I'm not a big gun nut and I don't even go hunting, but this I know from firsthand experience. If you carry a revolver, you may not even have to show it! Once they hear it and they know you're ready for them, they are just as scared as you. (Quote – You can discover what your enemy fears most by observing what he uses to frighten you!)

Muggers would rather just walk down the block a little farther and find someone without a gun to rob. Also, if you do have to pull the trigger, revolvers don't jam! If you pull the trigger, the bullet is coming. With a semi-automatic, that is not always the case. They tend to jam a lot, especially with a cheaper gun.

Here's another quick, funny story I'll throw in which relates to the topic we're on. After I received my license to carry, I went out to purchase a gun. When I walked into the gun store, there he was. This guy had gun nut written all over him. Short, round and burly! He was about 5'5," 200 pounds, 'Grizzly Adams' beard, cowboy boots, giant belt buckle, and a cannon that would put Clint Eastwood to shame strapped to his side.

"Can I help you?" he asked.

"Yeah, I'm looking for a gun but I'm not sure what kind I want yet." I answered while looking at the display cabinet.

"Okay, what do you need it for: home protection or self-defense?"

"Both," I said.

"Do you want to confront them?" he asked.

"I hope not," I said laughing. Well, this nut turns around and grabs a shotgun off the shelf. Real quick and hard he pumps the shotgun. 'Clink clink' was the sound it made.

"Do you know what that sound was?"

"Yes," I said.

"So does every burglar in America! If you hear somebody in your house, stand at the top of the steps and rack this bad boy. They'll run out the same way they came in and I don't even have to sell you the shells….you won't need 'em!"

"Yeah, that's great.... but I have a permit to carry. I don't think I'll get away with carrying a shotgun down the street." (Although I would like to.)

"Oh," he said, "that changes the gun but not the theory. Get yourself a revolver and, if there looks like there is going to be trouble, reach into your pocket and just crank the hammer back."

"Just crank the hammer back."

He was right! Little did I know that someday this crazy bastard was going to possibly save my life, but he did. He could have offered me a way more expensive semi-automatic, but he didn't. He gave me sound advice on why I should carry a revolver and it worked out.

I've been in the business as a Section 8 landlord for years and that is why you listen to my advice. This guy was in the gun selling business for years and that's why I took his advice. My point, if you follow somebody else's lead who knows what they're doing you're gonna end up on the winning side more often than not. An investment in knowledge always pays the best interest!!!

Let me say one more thing about guns and, I promise you, I'll try not to ever mention them again. Like I said, I'm not a gun nut. I don't go to shooting ranges, I don't hunt, and I'm not a member of the NRA. I simply carry a gun for self-defense.

Also, I'm not a preacher. I don't care what religion you are. I don't care if you're a Republican or a Democrat.... or whatever. I just enjoy talking real estate and real estate stories with people like you who enjoy hearing them! The next thing I'm going to tell you is the closest to talking politics that I'll ever get. It's about gun control.

If you don't have a gun permit and are thinking about getting one, do it now! With all of the crime and school shootings, this is one of our rights that Congress is going to make a run at taking away from us. If they don't take it away, they're going to make it almost impossible to obtain a permit to carry a firearm.

Right now, you only need a clean record and three references to get your permit. Soon there will be about ten hoops to jump through.......background checks, psychological evaluations, classes, etc. From what I'm reading, if you already have a permit to carry, you will fall under the 'grandfather act' which means you won't have to go through all the bullshit.

Sure, some people are for gun control and that's fine. Everybody has their own opinion on it and, since this is my book, I'll give you mine. Let's say they pass a law that nobody is permitted to carry or even own a gun. Anyone caught with a gun goes to jail for twenty years, no probation, and no exceptions. Well, I'm sure as hell going to stop carrying and turn in my gun. So is very other law abiding citizen but, guess who is not? You got it, the bad guys! Now, they'll have no fear of wondering what might be in your pocket. Things will only get worse.

Why am I so sure the bad guy won't turn in his gun? Because he's already carrying it around illegally! He's already not permitted to carry a gun but still chooses to even though it could land him in jail. He won't be any more illegal tomorrow than he was today.

If you want your gun permit, do yourself a favor and apply for it today. You might need it tomorrow! You owe it to you and your family to protect yourself. Life is worth living and if some creep decides he wants to try and take it from you, at least give yourself a fighting chance!

Story #2 – Rice at a heavy price! I ran into a fellow Southwest Philly landlord at a hardware store shortly after releasing Volume I. He told me he purchased my book and picked up a couple of good tips from it (shameless plug!) He told me he loved the water bill section but had not gotten around to removing hose bibs, washer hook-ups, etc. He told me all of his homes were already rented but, when a tenant moves out, he would be incorporating our systems. From talking to him, I knew he had a mix of about 30 homes in the area. Half were rented Section 8 and half were private rents. I wished him luck and was on my way.

About 3 months later, I was driving over to one of my properties. Suddenly, I heard a horn honking in back of me and a truck came ripping up behind me at about 50 mph. "Oh, man, am I going to have to yank this gun out for a second time?" was my first thought. Then this guy came pulling up beside me. It was the guy from the hardware store I had met 3 months ago. "Dude, you've got to pull over. I got a great story for ya!" I'm always looking for more book material, so naturally I pulled over.

I'll spare you all the 'he said', 'I said' crap and just tell you exactly what happened to this guy. He rented a house to a Vietnamese family who had no credit, good or bad. What they did have was cash and plenty of it. He told me he asked and received a six-month security deposit. They paid their rent early the first three months that they were in the home. He did notice that the water bill (which he had included in the rent) was gradually getting a little higher each month.

Another thing he noticed that was weird was every time that he stopped over the property, about six of them were working on the front lawn. Well, what is weird is the front lawn is only about 10' × 16'. They weren't cutting the grass, they were removing it and building a one-foot-high concrete wall around the outside of the lawn.

Finally, the fourth month's water bill rolled in, $347 bucks! The guy told me he couldn't get over to the property fast enough. You would not believe what they were doing. Growing rice!! Can you believe it? He told me they were irrigating the front lawn, keeping it under about eight inches of water. Of course he told them to put an end to the rice farm and that they would have to pay the water bill.

He told me that they did both and other than the rice incident, they were excellent tenants. You have to wonder what the hell is going on in some of these people's heads when they think of doing this kind of stuff in a property they are renting. You can go into a supermarket and buy a 100 lb. bag of rice for $20. Instead, this nut wants to feel like he's back home and grow rice on the front lawn to the tune of $347 bucks! What do I know...maybe it tastes better? This I do know; if the landlord would have capped the front hose bib, he would have never run into this problem.

Story #3 – Disposable stove! Nick and I were in the office when the phone rang.

"Mike, you've got to get over here.... there's an emergency."

"Oh, yeah, what is it," I asked.

"The stove...it's burning up!"

"Well, what the hell are you calling me for.... call 911 before the damn house burns down," I shouted into the phone!

"No, it's not on fire. Please, just come over here." I guess we were bored that day so we decided to check it out. Ya know, after being in this business for so long, you can almost sniff out a bogus call just by the tone of your tenant's voice.

When we got to the property, she brought us into the kitchen and proceeded to turn on the oven. "Give it about five minutes, you'll smell it." We only had to wait one minute. It smelled like somebody was boiling heads! I opened the oven door and looked in. This thing was pitch black with about an inch of grease on the walls and ceiling of the oven. "Do you smell it?" she asked.

"Yeah, I smell it and I'll bet half the neighborhood smells it." "Well, what are you going to do about it?" she asked.

"I'm not gonna do nothing.... you are!" I answered.

"What do you want me to do?" confused, she asked.

Nick chimed in with, "Try soap and water, lady!"

"Oh no, no, no, you've got to get me a new oven. I can't cook with this thing!"

This 'thing' that she was talking about was only eight months old! It was brand new when she moved in the property. "Lady, we don't install disposable ovens. You have to clean it!" Nick said.

"Well, I want a new one that's self-cleaning. How much more would it have cost you if you would have installed a self-cleaning oven from the beginning?" What balls, huh! Now she was really getting under Nick's skin!

"Look, you're not getting a new stove and I'm not even going to buy you a can of oven cleaner. What I am gonna do is call Section 8 for an emergency inspection to see that you clean this filthy thing before my house catches on fire!" You won't believe what she said next.

"Let me tell you something, that's why Section 8 gives you that little bit of extra money in your check. It's to help us! We're single mothers and we don't have time or money to do repairs or cleaning!"

I just about fell on the floor laughing (the floor was dirty so I stood and laughed). Anyway, here was Nick's reply. "What are you joking? A can of Easy Off costs about three bucks. Believe me, Section 8 doesn't put any extra money in my check to help you, they put it in my check to put up with you!"

Needless to say, she didn't get another stove and, to be honest with you, I don't know if she cleaned the one she had or not. She still lives there and we continue to pass inspections. I'm going to assume she either cleaned it or gave up cooking!

Story #4 and a tip! It's the little things that you do that really help make you a better landlord, like being prepared. One thing I've done from the beginning is to have my briefcase in the truck with me at all times. In it I carry some very important things such as a pen and paper to write lists, a flashlight, some business cards, and the Section 8 rule book to beat the inspectors over the head with. The most important thing that I carry in my briefcase is eviction notices! You never know when you'll need one. If I drive by a property with high grass, eviction notice! Drive by a property with an un-shoveled walkway, eviction notice! Drive by a property with a mass of people hanging out front, I think by now you can connect the dots. Anyway, these are the obvious times that you'll need an eviction notice handy. In this little story, it wasn't quite as obvious!

I received a call from a tenant who was a couple of days late on her rent. "Hey, Mike, I got your money. Can you stop over?"

"Yeah, I'll be there in about ten minutes," I answered. (Never tell them you'll get it tomorrow or the next day because a lot can happen in 24 hours.)

I shoot over to the property and knock on the door. "Hey Mike, come on in." As soon as I walked in, there he was…a pit bull puppy, cute as hell! I reached down and scratched him on his head as she filled out the money order. She handed it to me and said, "All right, I'm good until next month.

"Yeah, you're good. Just hold on a minute, I've got to get you something out of my truck."

MICHAEL MCLEAN & NICK CIPRIANO

She stood at the door waiting for me as I wrote away in the truck. When I finished, I walked back up the steps and handed it to her. "What's this," she asked.

"Read it, it's an eviction notice...but I guess you can't read because in the lease I had you sign, it clearly states 'No pets.'"

The nerve of her, knowing there are no pets allowed and then having the audacity to invite me over and let me right in. They just feel that you won't say shit as long as you're getting paid. Saying nothing would make the lease you had her sign a joke!

The price of exterminating for fleas, $60 bucks. The price of replacing dog pissed carpets, $1,200 bucks. The look on her face when I handed her that eviction notice, priceless!!!

Inspector was an Eagles nut! Story #5 – I told you in Volume I that if you're at all of your inspections, you might become friendly with some of the inspectors. Well, I did, except for one!

Everything started out great. He would cut me a break here and there and we got along just fine. This guy always wanted to talk sports. I love sports just as much as the next guy but this guy was over the top! If the subject turned to the Philadelphia Eagles, I couldn't get rid of him. I'd lay you odds that if he would have dropped his drawers, he would have Eagles underwear on! I would even try to fake it that I liked basketball. I knew enough to get by and, hey, if you're gonna pass me on my inspections, I might even wear a 76'ers hat. Truth of the matter is I can't watch basketball for two minutes. The sound of those sneakers squeaking and chirping all over the

SECTION 8 BIBLE, VOL 2

court makes my blood run cold and that's all you hear. Football, baseball or hockey, I can watch and talk with the best of them.

Anyway, it was a Monday and I had an inspection. That Sunday, the Eagles just got done blowing a 21-point lead and losing to the New York Giants. The inspector's face looked like it could have stopped a clock. You would have thought he was on the team.

"What's wrong," I asked. "Didn't you see the game yesterday?""Yeah, it was great! I had $500 bucks on the Giants!" (Football betting – don't get me started! That's a different book and a different story.)

"What, are you kidding me!?," he snapped. "You bet against the Eagles!?" I'll never forget the look on his face. I thought the guy was gonna try to square off with me in the middle of the living room.

"Buddy, don't take it personal. Next week, if the line looks good, I might be betting on the Eagles."

Well, betting against the Eagles must have been pretty sacred. I think he found about 20 things in the house that were wrong. This coming from a guy that as long as you were talking sports, he usually wouldn't even walk upstairs to inspect!

The next two times he came to inspect my properties, it was more of the same. I thought it might look like I was kissing his ass if I wore my Eagles jacket and an Eagle's helmet to the next inspection (and besides, if he failed me again I might have taken the helmet off and beat him over the head with it).

Finally, I lucked out with this guy. My neighbor, who had season tickets to the Eagles, asked me if I wanted to buy the week's up-coming game from him. The guy he usually went with had to work.

Also, they were calling for rain and the temperature to be in the thirties for Sunday's game. I bought the tickets off of him and waited at my property that Thursday for the inspector. I knew that if anybody would sit with a wet ass in thirty degree temperatures for five hours, it would be him!

"Yo, John. My neighbor gave me two tickets to this week's game. I gotta get a house ready this weekend so I can't use them. Do you want them?"

You would have thought Christmas came two weeks early. "You're kidding me, right?," he asked.

"No, I got them right in my truck if you want them."

"Absolutely, Mike! My son is gonna love this!," he said. I went to the truck and gave him the tickets. As he read them, his eyes got bigger and bigger. At first I thought it was the $100 price tag but, then he says, "Oh my God, these are podium tickets! It's supposed to pour on Sunday and these seats are under the podium!"

With that, he shook my hand and said, "Mike, I really appreciate this."

"No problem, John." He started dialing his cell phone and getting back into his car. "Yo John, did you forget about the inspection?," I asked.

"No, I didn't forget Mike…. you passed." I wouldn't say every inspection after the tickets went that way but there were no more twenty failed items either. The only thing that griped my ass was that they were podium seats that I gave him. I truly wanted to see him get soaked for breaking my balls on the previous inspections. Oh well, I guess you take the good with the bad. I'm not above a bribe and I guess he wasn't above taking one!

Another pit bull story, Story #6 – God help me with these dogs, I can't stand them! I don't know why tenants love these dogs so much but they do. I never get a call from Section 8 or neighbors saying, "Mike, your tenant has a Golden Retriever or a poodle." No, it's always a damn pit bull.

Well, I hear a knock at the office door and it's our mailman. I'm thinking since he's knocking on the door, he has a certified letter for me to sign. Instead, he spins around and shows me that the ass is ripped out of his pants.

"What the hell happened to you!"

"Your tenant's dog in 6308 Reedland Street tried to eat me. He didn't get skin but he did eat my pants!"

"Okay, and what do you want me to do?," I asked.

"Give me the $40 bucks to replace my pants," he answered. "I asked your tenant to pay me but she told me to come see you and get it. She said you'd probably turn it into your insurance carrier."

I gave the mailman $40 bucks and he was on his way. If I didn't, he would have tried to sue me or start delivering my mail at five o'clock. Now it was payback time!

I drew up an eviction letter and drove over to the tenant's house. "Pay me $40 bucks and get rid of that dog today or I'm getting Section 8 along with the mailman out here. The mailman's gonna swear your dog tried to eat him and Section 8 is gonna cut you off!" I yelled.

"That's not my dog, I was just babysitting him for someone" she said. These people must think you just fell out of a tree.

"I don't give a shit what you were doing but I do know what you will be doing…paying rent for the rest of your life if I don't get my $40 bucks back."

"I'll give the money to the mailman," she said.

"You'll do shit! You'll give it to me. I already paid the mailman. You're the jackass that had the balls to send him to my front door like this was my fault," I snapped back. Anyway, I'll make a long story short. She paid the $40 bucks (it was like pulling teeth), and she told me she got rid of the maneater.

About six weeks later, her annual inspection rolls around. I met the inspector outside the property and we knocked on the door. A kid about twenty-years-old answers. "Mrs. Shirley ain't here."

"I don't care if Mrs. Shirley is here or not. We've got an inspection to do," I told him.

"Hold on, before you come in, I've got to call her," he says.

"No you don't. I'm coming in. It's my house, not Mrs. Shirley's. She got a three week notice just like I did that Section 8 would be here today," I said as I walked into the house.

With that, the inspector and I started upstairs then hit the living room, dining room, and kitchen. In the kitchen, I noticed a dog bowl. This thing looked like something you'd feed Marmaduke out of…it was huge! Before I opened the door in the kitchen which led to the basement, I asked the kid, "Is it okay to go down here?"

"What?" he said. "I said is it okay to go down the basement?" "Yeah, it's cool," he returned.

I was still a little leery after seeing the dog bowl and, knowing the mailman almost got eaten alive, I just opened the door about five inches to peek down the steps. Next thing I know, all I see are teeth coming for my face! I tried to slam the door shut but ended up catching the dog's neck in between the door and the doorjamb. I leaned into the door with my shoulder as hard as I could and tried choking this monster out. At first, he was fighting and growling to come through the door but, the harder I squashed his neck in the door, the less he fought and he began to try and work his way back down the steps.

The inspector made a run for it out the front door (which I don't blame him) and the kid yells, "Let the door go, you're gonna choke him to death!"

Then I yelled twice as loud, "What the f*** do you think I'm trying to do?" Finally, after about a two-minute bout with this beast, he wiggled himself back down into the basement. I spun around and got right in that kid's face. "You simple asshole! Why didn't you tell me that thing was down there?"

"I don't live here and I didn't know," he said.

"Good, then get the hell out of here."

"What?" he said.

I yelled at the top of my lungs, "Get out!" At that very moment, if he didn't comply, I think I would have dragged him out by his skinny neck.

We immediately pushed for an eviction and won. We had the mailman and the inspector show up in court. Once Section 8 found out that the woman put one of their employees in danger, they threw her off the program for violating the lease. Just like I told her six weeks earlier, "You're gonna be paying rent for the rest of your life!"

Well, that's going to do it for my stories for now. I hope you enjoyed them. Some of them you can learn from and some of them were just some of my experiences. If you're in this field, believe me, you'll get some of your own. I hope you end up on the right side of all your stories and I'd love to hear about them. Drop me an e-mail if you get attacked by a pit bull, drag a twenty-year-old out of one of your properties by his neck, or find a rice garden in your front yard!

CHAPTER 7

LANDLORD STORIES

Alright, you've just read a couple of stories and experiences that Nick and I were involved in. Now, here are some stories that were sent to us from landlords from around the country.

Landlord story #1 – A landlord from St. Louis, Missouri dropped me an e-mail on what he thought of the book. He loved everything about it, except that we released it a couple of months too late. Here is his exact e-mail.

> "Mike and Nick, I just completed your book. I've been in the business for several years now and I must say, there are things in there that I never would have thought of doing. Although you guys removed garbage disposals to eliminate clogs, I found another reason to eliminate them! Unfortunately, I received your book a little too late.

"On January 2, 2007, I received a call from a tenant of mine. She informed me that her son was trying to release a plastic fork from the clogged garbage disposal. Well, he got the fork loose but he also lost the tips of three of his fingers!

Sink clogger and finger eliminator!

"What the idiot did was leave the switch in the 'on' position while trying to free the fork. The instant the fork came loose, the blades began to chop. (Sometimes I think the surest sign that intelligent life exists elsewhere in the universe is that none of it has tried to contact us!)

"Of course, I'm being sued. I have insurance and my properties are set up in an LLC, but it is still one big hassle. I'm sure before it's said and done, the kid will get paid and my insurance will go up.

"I just wanted to pass a story along to you and I hope it gets in your next book. Loved Volume I and can't wait for Volume II. Keep up the good work guys!"

John Glasgow
St. Louis, Missouri

John, congratulations, you made Volume II. I wish it could have been under different circumstances but, nonetheless, you made it.

I wasn't even thinking about the injuries a garbage disposal could cause! That's why I love it when I get a good e-mail. We can all learn from each other's mistakes so get those e-mails in here. Go to www.section8bible.com and then hit the 'Contact Us' brick.

Landlord story #2 – Ceiling fan puts an eye out and causes fourteen stitches! Here's another guy who got the book too late…also another injury. Here is Victor Arroyo from the Bronx, his exact e-mail.

"Mike and Nick, received your book on Friday and read it twice over the weekend. (Is this guy a speed reader or is my book too short?) I couldn't put the damn thing down! I loved every chapter but one, the 'Elimination' chapter'. Not that you guys weren't right on the money with everything that you told of eliminating, but I was so pissed I didn't order the book a year sooner. Here is what happened.

"A ceiling fan was in the master bedroom of a house that I purchased. The thing was practically brand new, so I left it.

Another reason to remove a ceiling fan is injuries.

"My tenant moves in and, for the first year she is there, everything is fine. Then I get a call from her lawyer asking me for my insurance carrier. I asked him what happened and here is what he told me.

"The tenant had two sons, one twelve and one ten. They were jumping up and down on the bed to see who could touch the ceiling first. What they forgot to do was turn off the ceiling fan! The twelve-year-old got up high enough that one of the blades, which was going 60 mph.struck him in the face. Not only did it rip him open (14 stitches), it put out his left eye.

"The case is still in court and, although I have insurance, I can hardly wait to hear the outcome, my nerves are shot! When I was reading your book and came to the part of eliminating ceiling fans, I wanted to kick myself in the ass. I had known about your book for quite some time but never got around to ordering it. Shame on me, I guess.

"If you can get this story passed along in Volume II, I would appreciate it. I wouldn't want something as stupid as this coming back to haunt anyone else."

Victor Arroyo
Bronx, New York

Vic, neither would eye, I mean I, (pardon the pun)! Anyway, your mistake made it into Volume II and I appreciate your e-mail.

Do you other landlords out there now see how this works? Give me something good that can help others and it will work for all of us. We are in this together and we can help each other out. It's us against them (the tenants and Section 8) so let's win this damn war! Give me a story, an idea, a theory. You don't need a ton of stories, just one that you think will be helpful or useful to others.

Readers are plentiful but thinkers are rare. I not only use all the brains I have, but all that I can borrow!

I have more respect for the person with a single idea who gets it there than for the person with a thousand ideas who does nothing.
(Thomas Edison)

CHAPTER 8

BAD NEIGHBORHOODS

Honestly, I never thought I would be writing a chapter on this subject. If I would have received the question of 'How do you know if you're in a bad neighborhood?' once or twice, I would have just bypassed this subject. However, I think I was asked this question about a thousand times. In this chapter, I'm not only going to let you know if you're in a bad neighborhood, I'm also going to make sure you don't buy a house in one!

Believe me, I'm not laughing at anyone who doesn't know what a bad neighborhood is or looks like. If you stuck me on a farm and asked me 'when do we plant the corn?' or 'how do we rotate the crops?' I wouldn't be able to tell you. It's the same for a farmer who is thinking about getting into real estate.

Right off the bat I'm going to tell you that if you are getting into real estate on this end, the neighborhoods you're going to be buying in are not going to be upper suburbia. Some crime you can expect as long as it's not too extensive. I whole-heartedly believe that low income housing is a safe as you make it. For example, if you go to work on your property at eight o'clock at night, after getting off work and after eating your dinner, and then stay up in the city until eleven o'clock, that's dangerous. If you go to work on your property directly after work, stay until seven o'clock and skip dinner until you get home, that's safe. Just as you create your own luck in life, you can also give yourself an edge when it comes to safety.

Okay, back to bad neighborhoods. Some of the stuff I'm going to tell you about bad neighborhoods is going to be kind of rough. Just revert back to the rules in Volume I: *'If you don't have the balls then don't buy the book.'*

If you don't know the neighborhood you're investing in, learn it! You should know every single street. You should know the streets you can buy a house on and you should know the streets you'd better not buy a house on let alone drive down! If you don't, maybe I can help explain them to you!

1. High Police Presence

If you see a lot of these around, it's not a good sign.

If you see a lot of patrol cars going up and down the street, you know the police are looking for something and I guarantee you it's not good. I think 'trouble' would be another name for it.

2. Corners

Always check your corners. If you see a lot of people milling around, lots of cars pulling up for a short period of time and then driving off, there is a pretty good chance that there is drug activity on the block. If you notice this activity, you can bet your prospective tenant will also notice. This will make the house hard to rent and I would not buy it no matter how good the deal was. I'm not saying the house will never rent... There's a home for everyone, but the longer a home sits vacant in a bad neighborhood, the more danger your investment is in. Not only is it not generating any money but those same people who are standing on the corner begin to notice your house is vacant. Not good!

And boarded up properties!

3. Board Ups

Not only do boarded up houses bring your appraisal value down, they attract bums. I'm not talking about your old wine-o on the corner that asks you for change, I'm talking about a guy that first rips all the copper out of the house and then decides to stay a while!

He's got other bum friends that he tells about the abandoned house that he's shacking up in and soon you've got about ten of them living there. How does that affect you? First, if you're working on a house close to a board up, they can either rob you or the tools off your truck. Second, they can break into your investment and strip it of copper and upgrades. Let's face it, they're in or around the boarded up property which they call home all day and night. You can't be at your investment all the time so they are going to get their shot at getting in. Third, if you're unlucky or stupid enough to buy a property next door to a board up, your property can go up in smoke!

Give these crack heads and bums some credit…they do know how to survive. One way to survive is by keeping warm. How do they keep warm in a house with no electric or gas you ask? Just like everything else in their life, they steal it! If your house is sitting vacant next to the one they are squatting in, they'll think nothing of breaking in and running an extension cord from your home into theirs. And guess what – you don't even have to be directly next door. I've seen them run two hundred feet of extension cord from the house they are staying in to another one four doors up the street. Now you've got one extension cord feeding an electric heater, a television, four lamps, a radio and, God knows what else! A fire can very easily start in your home or theirs.

Another thing they do is turn on the utilities illegally. They'll disconnect the gas meter and simply connect a six-inch nipple from feed to feed. Very dangerous! Now, they'll either heat the house with the heater if it works, or they will use the stove. I know that heating a house with a stove is dangerous because I've already lost one in this fashion. (see Volume I)

If you get a guy who thinks he is an electrician, he'll jump the electric meter.

Squatters will pull the meter, then run a small piece of copper from terminal to terminal to illegally steal electric.

What they will do is pull the electric meter off. Then they will simply run a three-inch piece of copper from terminal to terminal. Voila – let there be light!

If you get a guy (bum) next door that's not so inventive and is just looking for a roof over his head, you're still in trouble. Possibly more! First of all, he's dumber than the electric and gas thief because he doesn't know how to get the utilities on. So what does a jackass do when he's freezing? Like a caveman, he lights a fire in the house! I've seen them use a 55-gallon drum in the basement, burn a small fire in the kitchen sink, and light a pretty good one in the tub.

The best one I've ever heard was when they built a raging fire in a home that had a fireplace. Guess what? The fireplace was a fake! No chimney, no flue, just a fireplace mantel that was there as a decoration. It burnt the whole house down along with both of the homes attached to it!

Here is my rule of thumb. If there is only one board up on the block, I'll still make the deal as long as I am at least six houses away from it. If I'm getting a great deal on a house and there are two board ups on the block, I'll still make the deal but the same rule applies. (I have to be at least six homes away from the board up.) I won't make any deal on any street with more than two board ups on it, no matter how good of a deal.

Another reason not to purchase next door to a board up is for insurance purposes as in…. you won't be able to get any! That's right, insurance companies aren't fools either. They know the risks of insuring a property next door to a board up also. If you are able to find an insurance company that's willing to insure you, you're gonna pay through the nose for it.

Here are a couple of tips on what to do if you're not quite sure about a certain street. Maybe you're going back and forth on 'it's okay' or 'it's not okay'. The easiest thing to do is to ask a cop. If you see one walking the beat or driving past, simply tell him you're thinking about buying a house on such and such a block and you were wondering, 'how is that block?' Most will give you an honest answer that should help you make your decision a little easier. Don't be surprised if you get a sarcastic cop that hates his job and tells you, "The whole damn city is bad."

That's when you use tip #2. Simply go to the police station that patrols the street you want to purchase on. Go in and ask for a log of all the 911 calls within the past year that were reported on that particular street you want to make your purchase on. They have to and will give you a print-out of them. If the report doesn't look too bad, make the deal.

Remember, you're in the city so use your head a little bit. If there was a stolen car and a burglary, that would qualify as not too bad. Two burglaries, two murders and a shoot-out......see ya!

Location, Location, Location!

You've heard it a million times and when purchasing single family rentals in bad neighborhoods, it is and isn't any different. Sure, you want to purchase a house on a good block. Which is where it isn't any different. Here's where the rule of location, location, location is different when purchasing in the city.First, let's say you were buying properties in the suburbs. Your good and bad locations vary from town to town. We'll say a town called 'Springfield' is a great location to own a home. In most cases, you would have to go a couple of miles or a few towns over before you would hit a 'bad neighborhood'. It's not like that in the city! You might only have to go one block to go from a good street to a bad street. Sometimes it's like night and day.

This was the thing that blew me away when we first started investing in the city. On one block there would be no board ups. The houses would be well-kept and a renter would give his left arm to rent a home from you on this street. Go directly around the corner and you could find a street that looked like down town Baghdad! Board ups, burn outs, high crime, drugs, etc. It's the weirdest thing in the world that two streets so close to each other could be that opposite of each other. Our first office was located on the corner of the 61st block of Wheeler Street. It was a great location. Go out our front door and up one block to the 61st block of Glenmore Street and you would swear you were in hell!

6100 block of Wheeler, a terrific, safe block!

Very nice block just a stones throw away from bad block.

6100 block of Glenmore, a horrible block only 100 yards from Wheeler St.

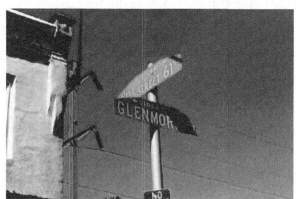

Run down homes on 6100 block of Glenmore Street.

The reason you really have to know your neighborhoods and its streets is so you don't get ripped off on the sale price of the home you're trying to purchase. Let's say you looked at a house on the 6100 block of Glenmore (the bad street one block from our office) which was listed at $50,000. The realtor pulls the comps (comparable price listings) for you and shows you that the houses only one block around the corner (Wheeler Street where our office was located) are going for $70,000. You would think, "Hey, I'm getting a great deal! I'm getting a house for $20,000 under the value!" You're really not.

What the realtor is doing in this situation is using the comps from the good block, which is only one block away, to support his price on the bad street. If you're sharp enough and know the neighborhood, a realtor won't be able to get away with that nonsense. You should be able to look at the comps and say, "I don't think so! Wheeler Street is a great block and Glenmore is a hell hole."

That is why whenever we purchased a house, we stuck by whatever the comps were on that exact street and block. I don't care if you're trying to purchase a house on the 6300 block of Elmwood Avenue and they give you a comp for the 6400 block of Elmwood Avenue. Disregard it! Only go by the comps that are on the exact block you're looking at.

More pictures of the warzone known as 6100 Glemore Street.

Porch roofs caving in.

And burnouts!

By my pictures you see how drastically only a few hundred feet can make a huge difference. Not only on a block, but also in your wallet!

There are so many decent areas to invest in and get a good deal in that I feel you may be setting yourself up for failure by purchasing a house for $20,000 in a bad location when if you look hard enough, you can find something two blocks away in a good area for say, $25,000.

Spend the extra $5,000 and save yourself the headaches of break-ins, vandalism and time. Yes, time! If you have a house that is on a good street, chances are the first time you show it, you'll rent it. Buy one on a bad street and you may have to show it countless times before it's rented. That means answering fifty phone calls, setting up showing times, driving over to the property to show it, and then finally hearing, "I'm going to look at a couple more properties before I make up my mind."

By purchasing the property in the better area for $5,000 more, you will also save cash! I'm going to give you an example of two identical, three bedroom properties. One is on a good block, the other on a bad block. The first thing that Section 8 will do after passing the inspection is give you a rating. The location of the house will affect the rating, so keep this in mind.

Let's say both of the homes are completed and ready to be rented by June 15th. The first looker to check out the home on the good block decides that they want to rent it. You fill out her packet and an inspection is set up for

June 20th. The inspector passes the property and gives you a rating of 7 (average). After the leasing department processes the packet they see that the fair market rent (average rent) on this particular block is $750. Since your rating was average, $750 is what you will receive. The leases are signed and by July 1st, your property is now rented.

Now, we will get to the property on the bad block. It's now July 15th. After showing the property twelve times you finally get the property rented. Same deal, the inspector comes out, you pass inspection but instead of getting a rating of 7, you receive a 5 because of the location. The average rent for the area is $750 but, because your rating was 5 (less than average), you only receive $675 for the rent. The leases are signed and by August 1st, your tenant takes possession of the property. Right off the bat, you just lost $675 because your property sat vacant thirty days longer than the property in the good location.

Now let's say both tenants stay in the property for five years (60 months).

Good Location Rent - $750.00 X 60 months = $40,000.00
Bad Location Rent   - $675.00 X 60 months = $40,500.00
Rent Difference = $ 4,500.00

Also, add in the $750 you received by getting the good location property rented a month sooner than the bad and your total comes to $5,250 .By purchasing the home in the good location, you made up the $5,000 difference in price, plus $250. Not only that, you will always have the luxury of getting the property in a good location rented quickly on location alone!

Final Note

When Nick and I started this business, we both had one thing on our mind. Volume! Obviously, the more houses we purchased, the higher the rent roll would climb. Most of the deals that came our way we either closed or tried like hell to close. But one thing we rarely sacrificed on was location. I would say 98% of our homes were purchased in and on fairly good locations and streets.

Just because you're doing 'low income housing', it does not mean you have to buy a $4,000 house that is on a horrible street and needs a ton of work. Real estate in the city is an amazing thing. Rather than buy a home with a horrible location for cheap, we decided to buy them in a good location, perhaps only a block away, for less than market value. It was these types of deals in which Nick and I made our move. If you look hard enough, use your head when it comes to searching the comps, use your balls when making your offer, you'll be able to do the same!

CHAPTER 9

FREE MONEY

Everybody loves free money! Stop right there. Nothing in this world is free. Even if you hit the lottery it cost you a buck to buy the ticket! The thing is, you start to hear so much bullshit about other landlords getting free winterization money, extra security money, free money or government bonuses to house low income families, etc., that you start to get jealous and also want a piece of the 'free money pie'. Nick and I are just as guilty as the rest of you. We took a couple of good runs at it, got lucky once, then called it quits.

By now, I'm sure you've seen that nut on television with frantic messages about free this and free that. You know him, the guy with the question marks all over his suit. Well, let me tell you about this nut....he's filthy rich and he didn't get that way from free grant money and government money! His name is Matthew Lesko and he became rich by selling books. He has published over seventy books and sold millions of them. His best seller was a book called "Getting Yours." Hey Matt, I'm still waiting for mine!

I'd be totally impressed if his books were free and he was a millionaire just by getting 'free money' from government programs. He didn't. He's rich from selling books. Nothing wrong with that! Hell, I hope I get rich from selling this book! I ain't gonna lie to ya! The difference is I'm selling a book on Section 8 land lording and I'm in the game. I live, eat, and breathe land lording. I guarantee you this guy has not applied for or received a nickel of government money. In fact, he's probably got to pay the government a couple of million in earned income taxes each year. The fact is, no matter what, the guy is wealthy. I guess I still have a sore ass from purchasing his book that I got no use whatsoever out of.

His book, just like all the 'free money' programs that we checked into was like chasing a ghost from the very beginning. You'd look up a grant program that was willing to give you $5,000 in grant money if you would use it for repairs on a home that you were going to rent to low income families and most of the time nobody would pick up the phone to return your call. If you were lucky enough to get a call back, it was one of two things.

#1. We need the HUD-1 settlement sheet, a list of the repairs you intend on doing, what they will cost, and when will they be completed. We will have to send out inspectors to check for lead base paint before any work begins on the property. Also, the inspectors will need to see everybody on the jobsite's license, their workman's comp insurance, blah, blah, blah.

You want to talk about red tape! They were opening up more cans of worms than you could shake a fishing hook at. I think I'd rather pay them the five grand not to come out to the jobsite! Section

8 inspectors, who are getting paid, love to break balls. Can you imagine how bad an inspector that's coming out to your job-site to give you money is going to break you balls? No thanks!

#2. 'Oh, sure, we can help you. First, you'll have to fill out an application that we can fax over to you. Fill it out, sign it, then send it back to us with a check for $125.' That's right – what a scam! They want you to send them money to "process" your application. Why the hell are you paying money to get free money? What a joke! It would be like me saying, "Hey, do you want my truck for free?" You would say, "Sure." "Okay, just fill out this application, give me a hundred bucks to "process" it and, if you qualify to get it for free, I'll give it to you.

If everyone was that dumb, I'd be rich. Your application would never get processed, it would hit the trash can, the hundred bucks would hit my bank account and the truck would stay in my possession. Then, I'd move on to the next sucker and do this again and again and again. Just as myscenario has scam written all over it, so did theirs.

The only time we were able to score some cash was with a 'winterization grant.' A guy from the Section 8 office was involved in it and picked one of our houses to participate in the program, so we gave it a shot. We were able to get ten new windows and two steel doors installed on the property. I'm sure the only reason we were approved was because the guy from Section 8 was involved. Had we gone at it alone, I'm sure the grant would have been denied.

It was one of those deals where you could only use the program once and it came with five thousand papers to sign. One of those papers came back to haunt us! One of the conditions of the winterization grant was that you could not sell the property for seven years, which we didn't intend on doing anyway. However, we were always jockeying different properties from bank to bank. Whether we were putting together blanket loans or refinancing properties, something was always cooking.

The minute we tried to put the grant property into a blanket loan is when the shit started. First, they thought we were trying to sell the property. After we assured them that we weren't, they informed us that they would not allow us to let the property be part of any blanket loan. In other words, "This was not part of the deal."

After looking over the stack of papers in the agreement that they had me sign (until my hand fell off), I didn't find anything that said we could not include this property into a blanket loan or refinance the property. We did it and they never said another word about it. To this day, I still don't know why they wanted to break 'em for us over this.

For the time, effort, and headaches that it takes to get a free grant, I'd rather earn it! They're just not worth the hassle. I'd just as soon find a great deal on a property, refinance it, and make ten grand. It's quicker and there is less stress involved. You owe nobody anything and you don't have to kiss anyone's ass.

If you know of a grant program out there that works well for landlords, let me know. Not only will I give it a shot, I'll pass the info on. That's what this book is all about, helping each other. Drop me an e- mail and, somehow, I'll get the information passed on!

CHAPTER 10

MANAGEMENT COMPANIES

Although there are some very good, legitimate management companies out there, I personally won't use any of them. I just feel that if you're getting involved in real estate, you might as well be hands-on. How else are you going to learn? If you lay the burden in someone else's lap, the answer is you'll never learn. Not only will you never learn, you'll never stop paying out cash!

Management companies want a percentage of rent collected, maintenance fees, repair costs, etc. They'll charge you phone time if they have to call the tenant, forty-one cents to mail your tenant a letter, and a buck to lick the envelope. Really, these are all things you can do yourself. Sure you're going to make a mistake here and there but you'll catch on. Besides, nobody, and I mean nobody is going to look after your money as well as yourself! When you're the guy working the wallet, you watch every penny and you see where it goes.

There are three different ways to get around using management companies. The first is if you're handy. Fix anything you think you can fix and if you're not sure, try to fix it anyway. Buy a 'how to' book or look up information on the internet. Most of the stuff, other than heaters and electrical, are pretty simple, common sense repairs. Some people are afraid to even attempt plumbing repairs but, I feel plumbing is very easy to learn. Not only is it easy to learn, you can't get hurt like you can while playing with electricity or installing a roof. I never took a course on plumbing and there is not one thing in a house that I can't fix when it comes to plumbing. Give it a shot and I swear you'll do alright. The worst that can happen is your job will leak. Shut off the main and call a plumber…at least you tried.

One thing I would do when I called a plumber in is I would watch him like a hawk. I figured, hell, if I'm paying him, I might as well get a free lesson out of it. Also, I wouldn't hesitate to ask him a question if I didn't understand why he was doing this or that. Sure your plumber is going to think you're a pain in the ass, but who cares! If this type of repair is needed again, you won't have to call him ever again.

The funniest thing ever said to me about plumbing came out of an electrician's mouth. He said, "Mike, plumbing is so damn easy it makes me sick. Do you want to know the three basic rules of plumbing?" Me, like a jackass thinking I might learn something said, "Of course." "All you have to know is shit runs downhill, don't bite your nails, and pay day is on Friday!"

I also had a plumber one day who was bitching about how little space he had while working under a sink. He was about 6'5" tall trying to fit his whole body into a 24" vanity. It was like trying to get ten pounds of shit into a five-pound bag. I said, "John, I don't think you're gonna make it." His reply was, "I'll make it. If I wanted an easy job, I would have become an electrician."

Everybody thinks they have the hardest job in the world, including me. The truth is, you can learn anything if you put your mind to it. The more you learn, the easier your job gets. Also, the easier your job gets, the more cash you will save!!

The second and simplest way to avoid the use of a management company is to pick up the phone!

A management company's favorite tool.

If someone calls you about a water heater that went bad, call three or four plumbers and get the best price. Once you get the best price, don't stop there. Now it's time to bullshit. Let's say the lowest price you received to replace the water heater was $375. Call the other three guys back and tell them you got a price of $350. One of them will bite and go lower, say, perhaps, $325. Then, call the other three back and tell them you received a price for $300. Work it down to the lowest bidder and then have him do the job. Use this technique on everything (heaters, roofs, floors, doors, etc.).

It is exactly what the management company is going to do for you. The only difference between you and them doing it is you won't see the savings if they do it for you. Once the management company gets to the lowest price, they'll tack on a hundred or so for themselves. You can do wonders with a phone and some balls! The worst somebody can do is say, "Sorry, I can't go that low," or perhaps hang up on you. That's okay because you have a phonebook full of people who may be able to go lower in price!

The third way to avoid management companies is to get all of your ducks in a row, which stems off the phonebook strategy. Once you've received the lowest price on a job, such as a water heater replacement, rubber roof or coating, heater installation, carpet replacement, etc., start creating a list. Simply write down the contractor's name along with his phone number, the job he performed for you, and what he charged. Here is a basic idea of what this list or chart should look like:

NAME	PHONE	JOB	PRICE
Dave Johns	555-727-1212	heater installations	$1800
Bill Stowe	555-724-8613	new service panel	$200
Bill Stowe	555-724-8613	installed service wire	$150
Daniels Plumbing	555-727-1616	installed new stack	$300
Joe Bitner	555-726-1123	installed rubber roof	$900
Glen Jackson	555-727-1414	installed new carpets	$10 per yard
Ronald Rickus	555-724-1515	hung 36 inch steel door	$325
Bill Newmiller	555-724-1616	installed and capped window	$180
Anthony Antonio	555-724-1717	pardged basement	$800
Harry Aungst	555-724-1818	installed iron railing	$60 per ft.
Rooney McKim	555-724-1919	painted house	$1200
Able Plumbing	555-724-2020	installed new toilet	$125
Able plumbing	555-724-2020	installed 60 inch vanity	$375

Soon, you shouldn't have to use the phonebook at all. If something goes wrong, simply revert back to your list. You've already shopped for the lowest price and, if the contractor did a nice job for you, keep using him. Soon you'll build a relationship that might last for years.

Finally, if you feel as though there is no way of getting around using a management company, shop them around also. Try to find the one that is going to cut into your profits the least, as well as one that's going to get you results. Like I said, there are some out there. You might have to go through ten of them to find one you're happy with but as long as you're willing to pay, there will always to somebody out there that will swear they can make you happy. Finding them is the trick!

CHAPTER 11

RESPECT

Okay, how many of you hate your boss? For those of you who answered, "I do," I guarantee you're at work fifteen minutes early and stay ten minutes late. I bet your lunch only lasts thirty minutes. You don't take sick days when you're hung over or because it's a beautiful day. When you really are sick, you fear calling him or her and telling them so. In fact, you may go as far as having your wife call you out!

Now for those of you who actually like your boss – today, you were five minutes late and tomorrow you'll leave ten minutes early. Friday, you'll take an hour lunch and, when you get back, you'll goof off for the last couple hours of the day. You know…. kind of get an early start to your weekend.

Monday, hell, everybody hates Mondays. You have no problem waking up, walking over to the phone, telling him you won't be in and then going back to bed. Let's face it, that's why you like him! He's a nice guy but you don't respect him. You can get away with murder and pay no consequences. You can complain and bitch when told what to do or what not to do and you won't get fired.

Well, it's the same with tenants! If they respect you, believe me, they fear you! If they break something, they're not going to be on the phone the instant it happens telling you that you have to get over to their house and fix it. In fact, they may even fix it themselves in fear of being evicted. You won't get calls when a door squeaks or a smoke detector battery dies. Their respect (or fear) of you keeps them in line.

With no fear or respect, I promise you, all hell will break loose! What can you do to establish your tenant's respect? I'll get into that in a minute, but, I will tell you this, you'd better get their respect from Jump Street. The second they move in is always the best time to go after it!

When your tenant looks at the property up until the time they sign the lease, you're the boss. The minute they sign the lease and you hand them the keys is usually when it will go south if you let it. Now they think they're the boss! They feel they are in the house and there is nothing you can do if they act up, the roles sort of reverse, if you will.

Put your foot down at that very moment and let them know they will never be your boss! Let them know you're in control and will stay in control. Cave into their first demand of "You gonna put a doorbell in here?" and you've lost it. Once you lose it, believe me, you'll never get it back.

Here is what I mean by caving in to their demands. I did touch base on this in Volume I but after all the questions I received, I'll go a little further into detail this time around.

Never, ever tell them (the tenants) that you'll give them something for free! In fact, act as though you're pissed off when they ask you for something that they want installed or could use. However, you shouldn't really be 'acting'. You really should be pissed! You didn't get into this business to make tenants happy and give away money and that's exactly what you are doing when you promise a tenant something that they can purchase themselves. Things such as a doorbell, which I'll bet I've been asked for over a hundred times! They don't wait long either. The minute you open the door after signing the lease, they'll stick their head back out of the door and ask or tell you, "You don't have a doorbell on here. Are you gonna get me one?" "Absolutely not, but you can get one at Home Depot if you want."

I've had some crazy tenants ask for a lawn mower to cut the grass. One asked me where the frying pans were that went with the stove! Another asked if I could install an alarm system and, how nice of her, said she would pay the $19 a month monitoring fee. When I was asked for big ticket items like the ones above, I simply said 'no' and laughed to myself that this tenants is nuts! When asked for the smaller ticket items that could fail you on inspections, such as smoke alarm batteries or light bulbs, not only would I say 'no', I would also get into their shit a little bit. I would shame, insult, and threaten all in one sentence so that I would never be asked to replace a .69 cent item ever again. Here is what the phone conversation would sound like. "Mr. Mike, the smoke alarm keeps on chirping. Are you going to come over and fix it before somebody gets burned up over here?" Right away I would feel my blood pressure skyrocket and I would jump right on them. "What, are you nuts? You want me to burn five bucks' worth of gas and a half hour of my time to replace a .69 cent battery. It's in your lease and it's your responsibility, but I would think that your family is worth more than .69 cents to you." They would come back with some half-assed excuse like they didn't know what it meant when the smoke detector beeps or they don't have any money right now. I would follow that with the threat of, "I don't care if that thing beeps for another year just as long as you've got a new battery in there come inspection time because, if I fail the inspection, you're gone."

I have finally come to the conclusion that some of these tenants are not crazy for asking for stuff, they're brazen! They have been so used to getting things for free and they just want it to continue and continue. I'll give them a safe, clean house to live in, that is not a problem. The problem begins when they want more than free and when it becomes more than free, you know who's pocket that it is coming out of, don't you? You've got it, yours!!! They really don't care what you think of them when it comes to asking for free stuff as long as they get it. That's where they are brazen. Well, I like to put the shoe on the other foot. I let them know they're not going to get shit extra and I don't care what they think of me! Once I pass inspection, it's done. Not another nickel is coming out of my pocket. If they break something, it's coming out of their pocket to fix it, not mine. Best of all, they signed a lease agreeing to my rules!

I'm sure you've heard the expression, "Give them an inch and they'll take a yard." Well some of these tenants will take a mile if you let them. The way to prevent it is so very simple. DON'T give them the first inch! Once they know they can't get so much as a light bulb out of you, they'll stop asking for stuff and that's the way I like it. If you give them something small and inexpensive and think, "What's a mini-blind gonna hurt?" well then, you've just made your first very costly mistake in this business. It'll be like a stray dog that you fed and now can't get rid of. Everyday instead of wanting something to eat, they want something to jazz up their house.

I love the movie, "The Landlord" with Joe Pesci. I hate Joe Pesci in it but I love the father. My favorite part is when he tells his son, Joe, "If you put so much as another light bulb in this place, I'll disown you." My kind of guy!

From day one I have accepted the fact that I will have to do repairs if I am going to be successful in this business. If someone doesn't have heat, hot water, or their roof is leaking and you don't fix it, you're not going to get paid. Not only that, your property will become run down. Believe me, when a tenant calls and says that their heater quit, it is not their fault and I'm going to get somebody out there as quick as possible to correct the problem. Other people who create their own damage and then want you to fix it, well, you know how I feel about that. I put tenants asking for things that they can afford just a rung above destructive tenants.

Let me try to drive this point into your head a little deeper if I haven't done so already. If a tenant of yours called and asked you for

$89, what would you say? Of course the answer would be NO! If you answered yes, you've purchased the wrong book.

Now let me camouflage that question for you, 'tenant style.' "Mr. Mike, can you get somebody out here to clean my carpets?" Some landlords would agree to this request and send a carpet cleaner over. Also, they would pick up the tab. Not me! In my mind, the tenant just asked me for an $89 hand out. I didn't dirty the carpets; they were clean when the tenant moved in and I don't have to walk or lay on them. When the carpets get dirty at my house, I don't call the mortgage company to get someone out there to clean my carpets. You have to take some kind of responsibility when you rent a home from someone and I believe the small stuff, like keeping it clean or changing a light bulb, should fall on the tenant. I'll handle the hard stuff like making the mortgage payment, paying the taxes and insurance, and major repairs.

I hate to sound like a smart ass but that's the way that you have got to be in this business if you want to make it! Every cent that you throw away to make your tenant happy is money you're taking away from your family. Don't fall for that 'you're rich, they're poor' bullshit either. Someday, I want to be rich! Some people get so rich they lose all respect for humanity. That's how rich I want to be. Carpets cost $89 to get cleaned and you're good for the year. That comes to about .25 cents a day. If your tenant doesn't want to spend a quarter a day to walk on clean carpets, why should you? Remember, remember, remember, you didn't get into this business to give away money. Get their respect and save a buck the first time that they ask you for a hand out. I don't care how you do it. Whether it's simply, abruptly, loudly, or obnoxiously! Tell them NO!

CHAPTER 12

LANDLORD TIPS

I must admit that I'm very impressed with the intelligence of my readers. Not only am I impressed with your intelligence but also with your slyness and ballseyness (is that a word?) Anyway, I'm sure you get the point.

I knew all along that Nick and I were not the only ones that were fed up with Section 8 and Section 8 tenant's bullshit! That's part of the reason why we wrote the book. I also knew that if we were getting creative, there were a lot more of you guys getting just as creative. In this chapter, I'm going to share with you some of the better ideas that were e-mailed to me from some landlords around the country. Although I received thousands of e-mails on who does this or that, I'm going to give you my top five. Believe me, I'd like to give you every good story but this is a paperback and I have to keep it under 200 pages!

If Nick and I chose your story, you'll be receiving a free copy of Volume II.

Idea #1 from Dale Miles, Detroit, Michigan

Dale gave me a great idea on how to protect your property while it's vacant. I know that in Volume I, we told you that you cannot use the double cylinder deadbolt lock.

Great to use when property is vacant!

They are a fire hazard and Section 8 does not approve of them. I argue with Section 8 on a lot of things but this is not one of them! I can totally see their point that if your house is on fire, you don't have time to look around for the key to open the front or back door.

What I suggested that you do while your unit is vacant was to throw a screw threw the back door or strap a 2" × 4" across the floor.

2 x 4 used to secure rear door.

This is a good idea that has worked for us for years. Sure, somebody can break in with a crowbar and pry the 2" × 4" off the floor but, hey, you take your chances. I also said that there really is not much you can do with the front door because you are going to need to get in and out of it. I was wrong! Somebody outthought me!

Dale told me that, although the double cylinder locks are illegal when your property is occupied, they are great to use while your property is vacant. The minute one of his properties becomes vacant, he simply switches the thumbnail lock to a double cylinder lock. When the unit becomes rented, he simply switches the double cylinder lock back to the thumbnail.

Remove thumbnail deadbolt when property is vacant.

This way, if crackhead Bob gets into your property through a window and disconnects the stove, he won't be getting it out the front or back door. He will be able to get the copper out of the window but he won't be making off with costly items such as your heater, hot water heater, stove, etc.

Good job Dale and, thanks!

Idea #2 from Albert Cheney, Denver, Colorado

Albert gave us the next great idea. None of his twenty-two homes had screens in any of the windows. There were two reasons for this, he told us. One reason was that up until January, 2007, you didn't need screens to pass your inspections. Then, Section 8 passed a new rule requiring all windows to have screens by April, 2007 in Denver.

The second reason was he found that when he rented a home, the screens were usually ripped or destroyed within a year's time! Spring would roll around and, like clockwork, the tenants would start calling and asking for new screens. Al found it easier to just remove (eliminate) all of the screens before the tenants moved in. Al, I like your style. Al put it into his leases that if the tenants wanted screens, they would have to have them made up themselves, at their expense!

When Section 8 made the rule change, Al went to his window manufacturer and asked the price to have the screens made up. How about $22 bucks a screen! Multiply that by about 18 windows per house and you're looking at about $8,712 not to mention the time you'll spend measuring every window in the house, waiting for the screens to be made, and then the fun chore of installing them.

What Al did was simple, slick, cheap and ingenious! He simply went to Home Depot and purchased stretch screens.

Stretch screen

They only cost ten bucks each so, right off the bat, the savings were tremendous. Plus, he didn't have to measure a couple hundred windows or wait for the screens to be made. The final bonus was how easy the installation of these screens were. Simply stretch the screen from side to side and you're back to passing inspections at a fraction of the cost.

Stretch screen in place

Al, we appreciate your suggestion and a free copy of Volume II is on the way!

Idea #3 from Michael Dunn, Newark, New Jersey

Idea number three comes to us from Newark, New Jersey. Mike Dunn dropped me an e-mail telling me I was wrong (how dare he!). Anyway, after reading his e-mail, I agree, sort of.

In Volume I, when I talked about getting the money you need to purchase a property, I said to stay away from using a 'seller's assist.' A seller's assist is when you ask the seller for money towards your closing cost and down payment. You can receive a seller's assist up to six percent of the sale price. (Example – if you were purchasing a home for 100k, you could ask the seller for 6k towards your closing and down payment.)

Anyway, Mike told me that he has purchased sixty properties in this fashion, without using a cent of his own money! Hey, if something worked out that well for someone, I have no problem putting it in my book. Also, Mike wasn't the only one who informed me that getting a seller's assist has worked for them.

I admit I could have been slightly wrong when telling you to bag the idea of a seller's assist. You've got to do what you've got to do to get the property you want. If this involves asking a seller for an assist, then take a shot at it! I must have shit luck because every time I tried this technique, it failed. It's really weird, I think a seller would rather you haggle him down on the price six thousand than give you a six-thousand-dollar seller's assist. Although it's the same thing and the bottom line comes out to the same amount, I believe they expect you to try and negotiate the 'asking price'. When you're asking the seller for something, they feel exactly that way....like they are being asked a favor by someone they don't even know.

I've heard sellers say, "Nobody gave me any money to buy this house; why should I give it to you?" Or, "How the hell are you trying to buy a house without a nickel in your pocket?" The bottom line is, if they have no other options or offers, they'll entertain yours. I guess you have to be in the right place at the right time. If it worked that well for other people, it can work for you.

Sorry, Mike, I'm still not ready to concede that I was wrong! I feel like I'm arguing with myself here on if a seller's assist is a good or bad idea. Like I said, if you throw the offer out there and get the deal done, it's a good thing. Here is where I still say it's a bad idea.

Let's say the seller is firm on his 100k asking price. You want this property so bad that you offer him 106k with a 6% ($6,000) sellers assist. You're still only paying 100k for the property and the seller is now happy because he's getting 100k. Now you have to keep your fingers crossed that the appraisals come back high enough to support the 106k sales price! If it doesn't, the deal blows up in your face and you wasted everyone's time.

The second problem I have with seller's assists is the mortgage companies. Not too many banks are going to get caught up in this type of lending. They know the score and more than likely, you're going to be using a B lender or finance company. That only leads to higher interest rates, higher fees, more hoops to jump through, and a longer time to get the deal done. The minute one thing goes wrong or delays, the seller can pull the plug and move on to a stronger deal (aka – someone with cash in his pocket). Again, you would have wasted everyone's time.

Seller's assists have worked for a lot of people so I'm not going to rule them out altogether. Just be careful when using them and keep a close eye on your interest rate and closing costs. Be sure no one tries to slip in any added fees.

Mike, thanks (I guess) for your e-mail and you'll also get a free copy of Volume II. If you think you've found something wrong in Volume II as well, you will not be permitted to purchase Volume III.

Idea #4 from Larry Greenwall, Atlanta, Georgia

Although this is more of a tip than an idea, nonetheless, it's still a great one! Larry informed us that he is a painter in the Atlanta area and owns several properties. After reading the painting section in Volume I, he agreed on everything that he read. He also wanted to add his own two cents to the chapter, so here it is.

"Mike, in Volume II, make sure you tell your readers to always use an inch and a quarter sleeve when rolling out the walls and ceilings of a house. Not only do they hold up and last a lot longer, they also hold more paint.

"The more paint a sleeve holds, the less time you'll spend reloading it (dipping it back into your paint bucket).

1 ¹/₄ sleeve holds the most paint.

"I know you guys always say time is money so tell your readers to stay away from the half inch, three quarter inch, and one inch sleeves. The inch and a quarter are the only way to go! For the extra buck you spend, the inch and a quarter will have you done in half the time.

"Excellent tip, Larry! Not only do the inch and a quarter sleeves work faster on walls and ceilings, they also work great when applying 'carpet in a can' to your floors!!!

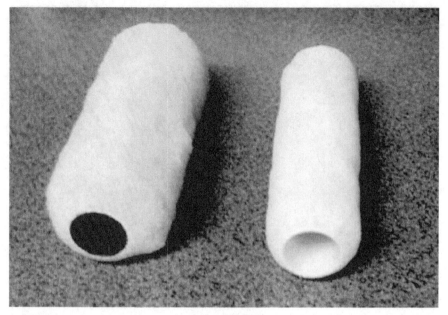

See the difference.

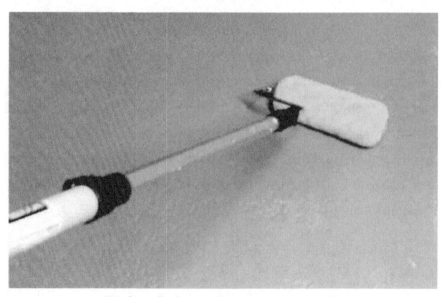

Works well when applying "carpet in a can".

CHAPTER 13

GARAGES

Garages and tenants are like oil and water. No matter how you mix them, they don't go together! Tenants will think of 99 other things to do with a garage rather than park a car in it. Let me give you a couple of examples.

I've had them make the garage into a fourth bedroom more than once. Also, they added a bed, television, sofa… the whole nine yards. The minute the Section 8 inspector sees that someone is occupying the garage, you failed your inspection.

I've had a guy running a repair shop out of one. That's right, just pull the car up, let him analyze the problem and once you settle on a price, just pull it into "Hakeem's Auto Shop." No bullshit, that's exactly what he called it! He even made a sign out of plywood with an arrow directing cars up the alley.

How about "Jerrell's Second Time Around." What's that? you ask. Well, Jerrell would trash pick old furniture. Then he would drag it into his store (better known as our garage), and sell it.

"Jerell's Dream"

"Gold's Gym!" Well, that's what it looked like anyhow. Think of a piece of exercise equipment and I'll bet you that this guy had it in the garage. I probably could have lived with that. What I couldn't live with is the fact that he had about 20 people lifting there! He only charged $15 per month to join his gym. How do I know what the membership fee was? Because, he ran an ad in the Philadelphia Review. He had his prices along with a coupon for two free workouts. What an entrepreneur!

If the tenants aren't using garages for business or living space, they are busy trashing them, literally! I can't tell you how many times a tenant moved out and, when we opened the garage door, we both said, "What the f***!" It always seemed like there was more trash and rubble left in a 10' × 15' space than what was left in the entire house. Now, you're stuck with clearing everything out of the garage, evicting the rats and roaches, and then spending your hard-earned money on dumping fees to dump someone else's trash!

Finally, I get a call from Animal Control. I'm thinking, "Did another pit bull eat the mailman?" I return their call and the lady wants to know if I'm the owner of the home on 25xx Hobson Street?

"Yes, I am," I answer.

"Who is your tenant," she asks.

"Why?"

"Because, he's running dog fights in the garage of your house!"

Can you freaking believe this? It got to the point that, if a house had a garage, we didn't even want to look at it. I felt like buying about twenty pit bulls myself and sticking one in every garage that I owned to keep the tenants out! My luck, the tenant would end up befriending the dog and he'd wind up eating my ass!

If I think about it for a little while longer, I'm sure I could come up with the 99 wrongful uses for a garage. However, I'm sure that by now you get my point. Now we had to come up with a solution to our garage problem. The way a Philadelphia row home is set up is that the garage is usually attached to the front or rear of the home.

Garage attached to front of property

Garage attached to rear of property

There is a connecting door in the garage that will give you access to the basement.

The first thing that had to be done before brainstorming was to eliminate the garage from the lease! That was not a problem until Section 8 came out to inspect. Their complaint was that the breaker box was in the garage. If a fuse blew, the tenant would not be able to change it or reset the breaker (not that they would anyway). Section 8 informed us that if the breaker box was in the garage, we would have to leave the garage in the lease so that the tenant would have access to it. That just blew our whole idea. Not so fast!!!

Unfortunately, some of the breaker boxes were located in the garage area.

"Let's just move the breaker box from the garage to the basement," Nick suggested. The price of having the breaker box moved from the garage into the basement was only $150 bucks. A great investment and worth every cent! We had our electrician simply drill a hole through the garage wall, rerun the electric line through the hole, and mount the breaker box back on the wall. It was $150 and no more garages, or so we thought.

Like I said, we owned row homes and all of the garages connected into the basement. There is a door in the basement that gives you access to go back and forth into the garage and basement. We put a padlock on this door and called it a day.

You let somebody rent a house off you and tell them not to enter a padlocked door, they're going to enter! Whether they tear the padlock off the door or remove the hinge pins, they're getting in. We would even show them that there is nothing in the garage but still, curiosity would get the best of them...curiosity or the fact that you told them to "stay the hell out of there!"

Now you've got to go back to the war room (our office) and come up with something else. What we did was remove the access door from the basement to the garage completely! Once the door was removed from the hinges, we framed out the opening with 2" × 4"s and screwed a half inch piece of plywood over both sides of the opening. For a final touch, we wired and stuccoes both sides of the plywood which totally sealed off the opening. On the front garage door, we added a hasp and padlock to each side of the garage door.

Padlocked garage door. You can see where the hasp was already pried off!

We weren't done yet! Finally, we drew up an addendum to our lease. It simply said that if the tenant entered or disturbed the garage in any way, they would be evicted. Ninety-nine percent of the time thereafter, we got our house back with a clear garage. Once in a while, someone would pull some bullshit like breaking a garage window and climbing in but, as long as they were not dragging junk into the garage, it didn't bother us as much.

By now you know how Nick and I are. When I say it didn't bother us as much, it bothered us enough and enough is too much! We had to come up with an idea that was fool proof, 100%! Sealing off the dividing door was working at 100% but it was the front garage door that was still annoying us a little bit. Like I said, if you padlock something, someone's gonna want to pry off the lock and see what you're locking up, even if it is an empty garage. Also, once in a while, somebody would break one of our garage door windows.

Garage windows can get broken, leading to failed inspections!

Although the tenant is responsible for repairing broken windows (part of our lease), sometimes the broken garage window was not found until the inspector did his annual inspection and, by then, it was too late!

Here is how slow my brain works sometimes! I was helping my brother put an extension on his house. He was knocking down the garage wall (which was connected to his basement) and extending the size of his basement. In Philly we say he was 'blowing out his garage.' I don't know what you say in your neck of the woods but I'm sure you get it; the garage was being eliminated to gain extra room in the basement.

Once we tore down the garage door and its tracks, we started to frame it out. He was going with plywood, siding, and a 36" steel door.

Go from this nasty, old garage door with broken windows

We finished, the job turned out great, and I went home and went to bed. As quick as my head hit the pillow, the light bulb went off! I sat straight up in the bed and said, "That's it! Rip off the garage doors and start adding a 36" steel door."

To this clean looking, sided rear door.

Another neatly eliminated garage!

No more broken windows or pried off padlocks. I couldn't wait to tell Nick so at one o'clock in the morning, I called him! Nick will talk real estate with you at two o'clock in the morning and if you have a good idea, he might stretch it to three o'clock. Anyway, this idea was added into our repertoire and our garage problem was solved. Now, so is yours!!!

CHAPTER 14

STREET SMARTS

'Street smarts' is a very important subject that I feel is usually under-rated. Most people think they are either invincible or lucky. Some don't even think bad things can happen to them at all. Most of the time, these people are right and nothing bad will ever happen to them. Me – I believe you create your own luck and destiny. Where you put yourself throughout the day and the situations that you put yourself in have a lot to do with it.

If someone gets lost and ends up on a horrible street, 99% of people know to keep moving. It's that 1% of people who stop and ask directions that end up a statistic. Stopping to ask directions in a horrible neighborhood is a pretty obvious situation that you don't want to know or put yourself in. However, when working on properties in the city, not all bad situations are as obvious. Let's talk about a few!

I'm not going to give you any made up, false examples of tragic events that happened to landlords. No, I'm going to give you six true stories of tragic events that have happened to landlords that I know personally. You can relax a little bit; no one was killed, so here goes.

Tragedy #1 – A Robbery

A landlord that Nick and I know pretty well was robbed of his wallet, watch, and boots! He was working on the property with the back door wide open. The guy simply walked in the door with a twelve inch steak knife, walked up behind our buddy and put the knife to his throat. He gave up his wallet and watch easily but couldn't figure out what the hell the creep was going to do with his boots. Obviously, he didn't need them for work but, the kicker is, our buddy is 5'6" tall and the robber was 6'2" tall. Either he had small feet or he sold the boots. Prevention – always lock all doors while working on your property.

Tragedy #2 – Another Robbery

Believe it or not, this story involves the same landlord. This time our friend was out front of the property, gabbing away on his cell phone. A guy walked up and just acted like he was going to walk past him and then, wham! He flattened him with a left hook. Our buddy went down and the thief took off with his cell phone. Prevention – number one, don't stand in the middle of the sidewalk talking on the phone. If you know you're in a bad area, either stay in your truck with the doors locked or get into the house and get the doors locked. Number two, always be aware of who is approaching you and never take your eyes off them. I'd rather hear, "Hey, man, you got a staring problem?" than getting decked by a left hook!

Tragedy #3 – An Assault

A landlord/contractor that Nick and I would occasionally hire to do concrete work was severely beaten half to death with a baseball bat. He owned a couple of properties and was in the process of cleaning one out when he made a near fatal mistake! He hired a guy who simply walked up to him and asked if he needed a hand. They both quickly agreed to an eight dollar an hour starting rate and the guy began helping with the clean out.

By lunch time, the guy had three hours in and asked if he could get a $10 advance out of his pay so he could get some lunch. The landlord agreed and like a fool, opened his wallet and gave the guy the $10. The guy returned after lunch and went back to work. Within 15 minutes, he snuck up behind the landlord and cracked him over the head with an aluminum bat that was in the property....not once, not twice, but about seven times! He not only wanted to rob him, he wanted to kill him. Prevention – never, ever hire a guy off the street that you don't even know! If I hire a bum to cut a couple of lawns, I know his name, where he lives, and if he has a criminal background. I don't need my head split open and I don't need the guy coming back later to rip the copper out of my house. You'll be surprised what a social security number can tell you!

Also, I don't even think I have to tell you this, never pull your wallet or any form of money out in front of a total stranger. To you, fifty bucks might not be a lot; to a drug addict, it's a fortune.

Tragedy #4 – A Strong-arm Robbery

A landlord that has been in the Southwest Philly area for years was forced to give up his wallet and wedding ring. It's a shame; this guy was 70-years-old and still owns three properties. He's already made his money and I think he just keeps a couple of properties to keep himself busy.

Well, he fell for the old, "Excuse me, do you know what time it is?" trick. The minute he stopped walking to look at his watch, they had him. Three of them surrounded him and told him to 'give it up' or they would punch his face in. Not a hard decision when you're 70-years-old. What a bunch of cowards! Prevention – never stop to give them the time of day! All they want you to do is to stop so they can get up on you. It's either, "What time is it? Or "Do you have an extra cigarette?" or some line of bullshit. Don't stop, keep on walking.

I hate to give out wrong advice and I'm not a criminal expert by any means, but I do sincerely believe that if you say something smart back to them, it decreases your odds of anything bad happening to you. Again, it's that 'respect' thing that I always talk about. I know that most experts would tell you to say nothing and keep on walking. My feeling is this – punks may and do take silence as fear. If I shoot my mouth off with something smart such as 'get a watch' or 'get lost', it kind of lets them know that I'm on to them. It lets them know that, yeah, I'm street smart and I know what you're trying to pull. They want to jump, rob, or sucker punch someone who is least expecting it or is afraid of them. Just by getting a little cocky, you're letting them know that you are neither. Hey, it's always worked for me!

Tragedy #5 – A Threat

I ran into a landlord that I would occasionally bullshit with at the

Section 8 office. While we were waiting to get our leases signed, we would talk about this or that or bitch about this, that, and the other. We got to be pretty good friends just by always running into each other down the Section 8 office.

Well, one day he hobbles in with a cast on his leg that went up to his thigh. Here is about how the conversation went.

I said, "Damn, George, what happened to you?"

"Mike, you're not gonna believe this one. I was capping a window from a 20' ladder and this guy comes walking up to the bottom of the ladder. He told me to throw down my money or he was going to yank the ladder down, with me on it! I told him that I didn't have any cash on me and he said, "Then drop me down your screw gun." I dropped it down to him and he still knocked the ladder over."

George ended up with a broken heel, fibula, and tibia. He was in a cast for four months and still walks with a limp.

Prevention – always have somebody foot (brace) the ladder. I'm not a big fan of heights so I always have someone at the bottom of my ladder anyhow. Also, I would have thrown the guy down about six slugs from my .38!

Tragedy #6 – An Almost Theft

Guess what? This one happened to yours truly! I worked a half day one Saturday and then packed it up for the day. I put my power tools in one tool bag and my hand tools in another, threw them in the back of my truck and was one my merry way.

I pulled up to a red light and on the corner sat about ten people at the bus stop. Well, one guy reaches right into the back of the truck and yanks out the bag of power tools! If, at this time, I would have had my gun permit, it would have made this situation rather simple. Unfortunately, I didn't have it yet.

What I did have under my seat was a two-foot crowbar. I threw the truck into park and jumped out with crowbar in hand. The nerve of this guy, he didn't even run! Either he thought I didn't see him take the bag, didn't care if I had seen him take the bag, or he thought I would be too afraid to get out of the truck and confront him. Anyway, I charged directly at him and swung the crowbar with every intention of splitting his wig open. He pulled his face back and I missed his nose by about a half inch. He immediately dropped the bag at his feet, held his arms wide apart and started yelling, "What's up, what's up!" To which I replied, "Your life mother-fucker if you come forward!"

His intimidation didn't work and I grabbed my bag and got back into my truck. Meanwhile, this jackass is now in the middle of the street yelling that I stole his bag! I was half tempted to throw the truck in reverse, run him over, and keep going. You just wish that one time they really did make a "Get out of jail free card." Ahh, I probably would have used it a hundred times prior to this incident anyhow!

Prevention – never leave anything in back of your truck that is not locked down. Also, it doesn't hurt to have something in the cab of your truck to protect yourself with. I know a guy who carries around a baseball bat and glove. He hasn't played baseball in years but as long as the glove is with the bat, he's in good shape if he gets pulled over by the cops. I told him just don't get pulled over in the dead of winter!

My final thoughts on street smarts – if you don't have them, you can easily establish them. It's common sense really. A kid that is born and raised in the city will have them by the time he is eight years old. As long as you're smarter than an eight-year-old, you'll have no trouble getting some street smarts. Also, lucky for you, we wrote a book that gives you quite a few good tips before you even step one foot into the world of Section 8 landlording!

Always remember to stay alert, watch your front and your back, and trust no one. Most likely, nothing will happen to you and you'll make out just fine. However, if a situation arises, I hope that I have prepared you. You can make all the money in the world but if you're not around to enjoy it, what good is it? Safety first!

CHAPTER 15

ORGANIZATION

Throughout Volume I and Volume II, I have told you this or that saves time and money. Time, as well as money, is a very valuable thing that you can never have too much of. In my mind, wasting time by being disorganized is the worst mistake one can make! *Lost time is never found again* (Ben Franklin).

Everybody is given the exact amount of time, which boils down to twenty-four hours a day. How you use this time throughout the day will determine if you're home by four o'clock to eat dinner with your family or if you're sitting in rush hour traffic at five o'clock, bitching and wishing you could have been done doing whatever it was you were doing an hour sooner.

Of course you're going to run into unforeseen problems now and then, such as a broken water heater at three o'clock or the front door that you're in the process of hanging won't cooperate and you end up getting home later than anticipated. Those type of problems you can live with because there is nothing you can do to prevent them. They are not the problems I'm talking about here.

The type of problems that could have been prevented are the problems I want to discuss. You know the ones, like searching for an extension cord in your shop, or trying to find the keys to one of your units, or running out of a product that you use all the time (like stick down tiles) and having to run to Home Depot. These are all problems that could have been prevented and end up wasting time.

Just look at the three problems I described. Let's say searching for the extension cord took fifteen minutes, finding the keys took ten minutes, and driving back and forth to Home Depot to get a box of tile took forty minutes. You just lost over an hour of time. It's little horseshit problems like this that you run into every day that end up costing you time and can easily be prevented.

If you would have had a hook for your extension cords to be hung on, a board for your keys to be hung on, and a good supply of materials that you generally use, you wouldn't have lost a minute.

*Extenson cords
neatly hung
(our shop)*

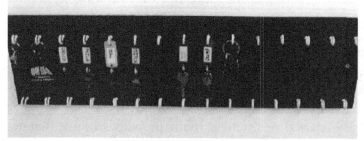

*Organized
keyboad
(our office).*

I have been in plenty of other landlord's shops or offices and I don't know how they find a damn thing. When I told you not to be that landlord who has to root through a box of fifty keys just to find the set he's looking for, I wasn't making this up as an example! A landlord that I'm pretty good friends with is the guy that I'm talking about here. Not only are his keys disorganized, everything that he owns is disorganized. His tools, his stock, his paperwork, and his life! It became a very bad habit.

When I question him on why he's such a slob, he tells me it's a bad habit that he got himself into years ago and just can't get out of. I disagree. I just think he's a lazy slob! I bet he wastes about ten hours a week just looking for things. I kid you not, his keys are kept in a Nike shoebox and half of them don't even have a tag on them. Half of his tools are in his office, a quarter of them are strewn about in his truck, and the last quarter of his tools are either in his vacant units or missing. I must have one of those mental conditions or an obsessive/compulsive disorder because whenever I stop by his office, I feel like I should start organizing and putting stuff away. Then the better half of me takes over then says, "If this guy wants to live and work like a pig, go right ahead."

I've run across a lot of landlords who run their business the same exact way, so this guy is not the only one. I can walk right into someone's shop or office and within ten seconds I can tell you if they have their shit together or they're a lazy bum. The thing that drives me nuts about the whole problem is that it doesn't take money, space or time to be organized. In fact, it takes more time to be disorganized! We started out with a room in Nick's house that we used as our office and a garage that we used for our materials. We built shelves in the garage and utilized every inch of space that we had. In the office, we had a homemade key board and a filing cabinet. That's right; we didn't use a computer to keep track of our properties, just a filing cabinet! And guess what? We still only use a filing cabinet. The minute we purchase a home, we make up a new file and place it in the filing cabinet.

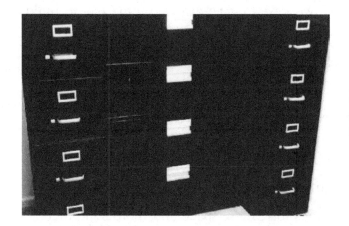

Huge filing cabinet that we use.

Any receipt, lease, insurance binder, etc. will go directly into its proper folder. We just feel it's easier to put something away rather than scanning everything and loading it into the computer.

Receipts are placed into folders.

As far as stock went, anything that we used a lot of, such as tile, luan, screws, doorknobs, etc., we purchased twelve of. Other items that we didn't use a lot of (toilets, sinks, stoves), we kept only one or two of. It took us two days to get organized. One day to build the shelves in the garage and a second day to purchase the stock and load it onto the shelves!

At the end of every week we would take an inventory check and sometime over the weekend, we would pick up whatever it was we were low on. Now, instead of going to Home Depot a dozen times throughout the week, we were just going once over the weekend.

Soon after getting up to the forty house range, we realized that we needed more inventory, more space and more equipment. Also, in order to be more organized, we wanted our shop and office to be in the same building. We lucked out by finding a building that was once used as a bakery.

This building was once a bakery. It became our shop.

Side of building

The upstairs we made into our office and the basement, which was huge, now became our shop.

Once again we began building shelves and stocking material. Soon we had a mini-hardware store in our basement. Supplies and materials were kept on one side, equipment and tools on the other. It was so much easier to run back to the shop, which was directly in the middle of the neighborhood we were buying in, than to head to Home Depot which was twenty minutes away.

Here we grow again! That's right – by the time we reached the 120 house plateau, we felt the rope tightening around our necks again. What happens is you want to keep enough material on hand for forty or fifty houses and before you know it, you're up over one hundred homes. If you want to keep growing your business, you've got to keep expanding. If you don't, you quickly run out of room. What happens when you run out of room? You start becoming disorganized! Not only that, you start to run out of materials a lot faster.

When you had forty houses, the two toilets you have in stock may hang around for a month or so. When you get up to one hundred houses, you're purchasing about five or six new houses a month, and those two toilets aren't going to last a week! It was time to make another move and that is exactly what we did.

This time we said we're going to do it right. We'll find a building that we won't run out of space in, something that is gigantic and will let us grow and grow. We found that building but it was nothing like we had envisioned.

Every factory or warehouse that we were shown, had an asking price that started around 300k. The more time we spent looking, the more congested our 'basement shop' became. We had to pull the trigger on something and, finally, we did!

"What a hell hole!"

Bathroom

What you are looking at above was our 'state of the art' shop. It was hands down the dirtiest, filthiest, disgusting building we ever stepped foot in. So we bought it! At one time it was a repair garage but it had been vacant for years. The guy that owned it had just been released from prison and needed some fast cash to get his life started again. He was asking 250k because, when completely rehabbed, the building would appraise for 400k. We offered 90k and he accepted the offer. Honestly, I didn't know who was getting the better end of the deal.

Office area

We started with the clean out.

Before beginning work on it, I think we had to throw out every crackhead and hooker in Southwest Philly. Once they were gone, the work began.

We removed the rat's nest of an electrical system.

We stripped everything down to the bare walls. The plumbing and copper were already gone, (gee, I wonder where that went?) and we also removed every single wire in the place. We installed a completely new roof, heater, electrical service, plumbing, etc. We ended up putting 60k into the place but, by the time it was finished, it truly was a state-of-the-art shop!

We removed over 200 old tires.

We removed tons and tons of old car parts.

We finally had it emptied.

Then we started framing up the inside.

We began getting the outside in shape.

The stucco scratch coat is going on nicely

Now, it's really coming together!

From a hell hole to paradise!

Now it was time to stock it. This time instead of building shelves, we purchased them. You can only get so much stock onto a wooden shelf before it begins to get congested. What we did is find out where Home Depot gets its shelving and we went out and purchased the same exact thing.

Heavy duty shelving holding a bunk of plywood and luan

Hey, if you want to make money in this business, sometimes you've got to spend a little. Now, instead of having five sheets of plywood in stock, we bought a bunk of plywood and had one hundred sheets in stock. Instead of two toilets, we had eight. Instead of, well, you get the picture! I also hope you get the point. If you're serious about getting your volume of houses up, don't be afraid to expand your business. You need a place where you can fit everything comfortably.

Heavy duty shelving holding doors and hopper windows.

Shelf holding 2 x 4's.

A pipe rack holding ¹/₂" copper and PVC.

A trim rack holding all sorts of trim, baseboard, and molding.

Hooks neatly holding shovels, rakes, and brooms.

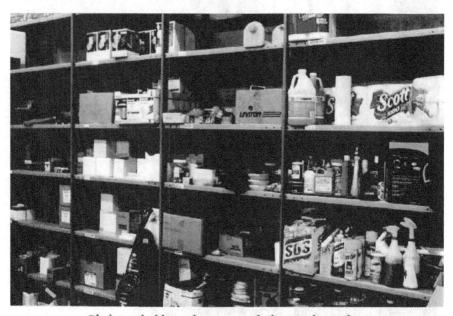

Shelving holding cleaning and electrical supplies.

More cleaning supplies.

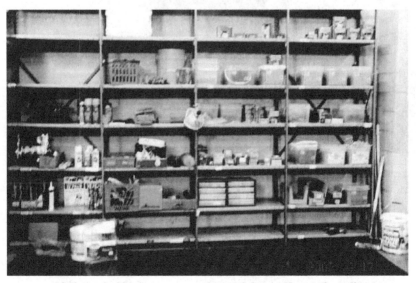

Shelving holding screws, nails, stickdown tile, and caulk

Pegboard holding hardware supplies.

Always aim and set your sights high, higher than you can even imagine. If you accomplish what you set out to do, aim higher! Once you've got the correct, organized setup, nothing will be able to stop you. You'll be a house turnover machine. Whether it's a well-stocked garage that you're running twenty houses out of or a 7,000 square foot factory that you're running three hundred houses out of, always stay organized and I promise you, your business will continue to grow and grow!As you can probably tell by now, I love using quotes to get my point across. Some great men and women have said some pretty smart things, and when you put them together, you get a famous quote. I'll end this chapter with what some of them said about 'time and organization'!

We must use time as a tool, not a crutch. (JFK)

Time is the coin of your life. It is the only coin you have, and only you can determine how it will be spent. (Carl Sandberg)

Time is what we want most, but we use worst. (William Penn)

Until you value yourself, you won't value your time. Until you value your time, you will do nothing with it. (M. Scott Peck)

You may delay, but time will not. (Ben Franklin)

Much may be done in those little shreds and patches of time which everyday produces, and which most men throw away. (Charles Colton)

Day – (noun) A period of twenty-four hours, mostly misspent. (Ambrose Bierce)

Organizing is something you do before you do something, so that when you do it, it's not all mixed up. (A.A. Milne)

To be powerful, you must be strong, and to have dominion you must have a genius for organizing. (John Newman)

Science is organized knowledge. Wisdom is organized life.
(Immanuel Kant)

Don't agonize. Organize!!! (Florynce Kennedy)

CHAPTER 16

CODE AND RULE CHANGES

Nothing annoys me more than a code or rule change! You have been doing a certain thing one way for years. Then, all of a sudden, it's not good enough anymore. Section 8 decides they want you to do it a different way. Some chief or head of inspections decides that something can be made safer or a tenant gets hurt on a specific item in the house and all hell breaks loose. You'd like Section 8 to send you out a memo, an e-mail or anything and tell you that starting in sixty days, this or that will no longer be accepted. However, that's rarely the case.

You're usually informed when the inspector comes out to inspect your property and says, "Mike, I have bad news. We can no longer accept not having a GFI outlet in the bathroom." Ten dollar items or repairs, such as switching a regular outlet over to a GFI, or installing a GFI, I can accept. The minor stuff that isn't going to cost you a ton of cash, although I don't like it, I can deal with. It's when Section 8 tells you that you have to start switching, changing, or eliminating products or fixtures in the house that are rather expensive is when I hit the roof.

Here is an example. The houses that Nick and I purchase are usually about 80-years-old...nothing you can do about it. Ninety percent of the houses in Southwest Philly were built in the 1920s. Eighty years ago, they used an exterior basement door that was 1 3/8" thick. Nowadays, an exterior basement door is 1¾" thick.

When we would rehab our properties, we would always get rid of the eighty year-old door and install a new, exterior basement door. The old basement doors had six to nine small glass windows, (which could easily break and cause you to fail inspection) were painted with lead base paint, (which could cause a lawsuit and fail you on inspection) and the wood was usually starting to dry rot (which could also fail you on inspection). Not to mention that if you wanted the damn thing to lock, you would have to add a slide bolt lock because 10 to 1 odds, the skeleton key lock wasn't working.

Exterior rear doors that we would replace with new door.

Bottom line, it was just easier to add a new door and Kwikset lock. Sounds easy enough, hang a new basement door and you're good, right? Wrong! Try finding a 1 ⊠ exterior door. It's impossible. Either they stopped making them or the State of Pennsylvania outlawed them because we can't find one anywhere. The problem is that the only door that the jamb would accept was a 1 ⊠ door. The only size exterior door they make (or we could find) was 1 ¾." Now, we had a dilemma.

Either rip out the entire jamb and install a 1 ¾" pre-hung steel door or, figure something else out that was easier and cheaper. You know how much I love easier and cheaper, so that's the route we took.

Home Depot sold a 1 ⊠ solid interior door that we used on all of our bedrooms.

→
Door after being painted with exterior paint.

The only thing that the rule book said was that the exterior basement door had to be was a 'solid core' door. The rule book said nothing about thickness. How do you make a solid interior door into an exterior door? Easy! Throw a coat of exterior paint on it and add a door sweep to the bottom.

That is exactly what we did and used on about 150 of our properties basement doors. Hey, the door was solid, we put a new lock on it, it didn't have those nine windows that somebody could put a fist through and break in, it was much safer than that eighty-year-old, dry- rotted, original door and the best part was it passed inspection!

Well, finally some asshole inspector who must have taken a class on carpentry figured it out. "Mike, this is an interior door. I can't pass you with this."

At first, I tried being honest and nice. "Jim, I know it's an interior door but the thickest door the jamb will accept is 1 ⊠ Anything else and I would have to rip the entire jamb out."

"Yeah, that's what I want you to do," he said.

"What are you crazy? I must have already installed over 150 of these doors and I have been passing my inspections for years!"

He just looked at me and said, "Oh, I'm not going to pass any of your houses that have this type of door installed." Enough being nice, now I freaking lost it.

"Hey, Jim, you know the two houses you inspected for me on Tuesday and passed? Well, they both had these identical doors. And let me tell you something else, I think you're breaking my balls! You and I both know that the doors I'm using now are 100% safer than the piece of shit that was on here which, by the way, I should have just left the hell on here."

"Yeah, I know Mike, but this is still an interior door." Obviously, there was no getting through to this jerkoff, but I figured I'd try one more time.

"So let me get this straight. Instead of ripping off the lead infested, eighty-year-old door that doesn't lock and replacing it with this brand new solid door that does lock, you'd just rather me leave the old door?"

"Well, the old door is an exterior door," he replied. "What the f*** is the difference? They're both solid 1 ⊠ doors," I screamed.

He couldn't give me an answer and he wasn't going to pass me. All I could think about was the other 150 doors that I installed at about a hundred bucks a pop, would now be failing inspections...150 × $100 = $15,000! It would be cheaper to put a hit out on the inspector but I didn't feel like sitting in jail for the rest of my life. Also, there is a good chance I could run into some of my ex-tenants in there so I had to rule that out!

The first thing I tried to do was go over the inspector's head. I went to his boss and told him that I'm already 150 doors deep into this 'door adventure' and a midstream rule change would cost me a small fortune. Also, I wanted to explain to him how dumb it would be to start ripping down perfectly good doors. He was having none of it!

"Mike, I'd like to help you but Jim (the jerkoff inspector) is pretty hell-bent on you using a solid core door."

"For the last damn time," I snapped, "the door is solid!"

"Well, Mike, that's not what Jim is telling me. He's telling me that you're using an interior door where we are calling for an exterior door."

"The only reason that it's being labeled an interior door is because it does not have a finish on it. The door will warp or rot if you don't paint it with exterior paint to protect it. Believe me, every door I have installed has been painted with exterior paint."

"Sorry, Mike, I've got to go with Jim on this one."

Just when I was about to admit defeat and start ripping down about 150 doors, I thought to myself, let me check this rule book one more time. There it was under exterior doors. "All exterior doors must be of solid core." Well, a solid core door was exactly what I was using. The rule book never made mention or specified that an exterior door had to be 1 ¾."

I got into my truck and headed back down to the Section 8 office for round two of arguing. This time, I had an ace up my sleeve...more like a door in the back of my pickup! That's right, I loaded the exact door we were using into the back of my truck and brought it down to the Section 8 office with me.

As soon as I walked in the office door, I could see the look on the head of inspections' face. It was that of disgust like, "Oh no, here comes this pain in the ass again." But you know what? I don't really give a shit about what he or anybody else that is trying to cost me 15k thinks about me! If the shoe were on the other foot and I was trying to put him out 15k, you'd better bet your life he'd be a pain in my ass. I wouldn't expect anything less.

"Kevin, I was wondering if you could do me a favor before I start ripping down all of those doors."

"What's that Mike?" he asked. "I was wondering if you could put a 'grandfather clause' in. You know, let me slide on the doors I already installed and from now on, I'll start installing steel doors."

I already knew he was going to say no, but this was part of the set-up. We have had some rules 'grandfathered' in the past but this one wasn't going to be one of them. Either this wasn't my day or this guy had a wild hair up his ass and it went something like this.

"Can't do it, Mike. It's too dangerous to have an interior door out back. It's hollow and somebody can very easily kick it down. You need a solid door and we're not making any exceptions." Bingo, I got 'em! Now it's time to finish the set-up just to be sure that there's no miscommunications.

"Alright, alright, Kevin, I'll use a solid core door. But can it be 1 ⌧ solid door because that's the only size door that I can attach to the jamb?"

"Mike, I don't care what kind of door you use just as long as it's solid," he said. I knew he wanted to get rid of me so I figured I'd pester him a little bit more.

"Hey, I'm parked out front and I have the door that I intend on using in the back of my truck. Do you think you can run out front really quick just to okay it? I don't want to be ripping down anymore doors if this one's not up to your satisfaction" I needled.

Boy, sometimes I can be a sneak. I'm a sneak as much as they're ball breakers. Sometimes, you've got to play a little dirty with the inspectors also! After all of my failures in trying to get these guys to see things my way, they thought I had given in. However, my failures are rarely complete failures; they're more like future investments. We walked out front, I let down the tailgate and he lifted the door out of the bed of the truck and then knocked on it.

"Yeah, that will do, it's solid."

"Good, I'm glad you think so because it's the same door that I have been using for the past seven years," I said. Well you could hear crickets chirping. He was dead silent as he stared at me for about ten seconds. I thought he was going to splinter the door over my head. Then, something really weird happened as a slight grin came over his face. "You son of a bitch, you got me." Then, I even started laughing.

"Well, Kevin, what do you expect? I've been telling you guys all along that the door was solid but Jim's too busy breaking my balls and trying to cost me 15 grands. He should be failing the slumlords that leave the hundred-year-old doors in place, not me!"

"Mike, enough said. The door is solid and that's the only thing the rule book requires. Anybody who suckers me that good deserves to pass anyhow. I'll tell Jim the doors you're using are fine, you're good."

I bet you, I laughed the entire ride home. Honest to God, I'm even laughing right now as I'm writing this down! If you could have seen the look on his face when I told him that the door he is knocking on and 'okaying' was the same door he was failing me on five minutes ago. Priceless!

There is a moral to this story, other than the head of inspections is a sucker. One way to beat a rule change that's going to cost you a ton of cash is to argue. Argue with everything you've got and don't worry about what anyone thinks of you. Let them know you're pissed about them trying to take money out of your pocket. Ask them to 'grandfather' a rule change, make an exception to the rule, whatever it takes to pass.

They like to act like their hands are tied but they're not. I've been through a hundred inspectors and I've seen several 'heads of inspections' come and go. Somewhere, somehow, or at some time, they have all cut me a break! Persistence is the key. Once you establish just how much a pain in the ass you can be, you will begin to see things loosen up. You'll start to get cut more and more breaks.

Another way to get around a code or rule change is to simply adjust or outthink them. It's usually not that hard. It's really like a game of chess; they make a move and you nullify it. Usually the guy making the rule change is not out in the trenches so this makes it a whole lot easier. You want another example, don't you? Okay, here goes.

I told you in Volume I that you need a railing going down any staircase over thirty-six inches. I also told you how the railings going down the basement steps would always disappear. A railing is something that you grab onto if you're falling down the steps; any idiot knows that. Well, railings go for $2.50 per foot and 2" × 4"s go for .28 cents per foot. Instead of using railing, we used 2" × 4"s. What's the difference, we thought. If you lose your footing, you're going to grab onto a 2" × 4" just the same as you would grab onto a railing. When we first started out, we did use railing. However, it always seemed to get ripped down and nobody knew where it was come inspection time. Anyway, back to the story.

An inspector named Dobbs came out to one of our properties to do an annual inspection. This guy was a jerkoff's jerkoff! He wore the badge, the hat, the tool belt, and he even carried a small nightstick. I didn't know if he was gonna arrest me or inspect my house. Right away, I knew I was in trouble.

As he walked down the basement steps, he asked, "What's this?"

"It's a railing, what does it look like?" I said.

"Uh, excuse me, I ask the questions around here."

I guess he wanted me to say, "Yes, officer."

"This ain't no railing, it's a 2" × 4" screwed to the wall. I want it ripped down and replaced with a railing," he said. Now it was my turn.

"Unfortunately for you, I won't be doing that. I told Kevin (the head of inspections) that our railings keep disappearing and that we were switching to 2" × 4"s. Kevin said it was fine and I've been using 2" × 4"s as railings for two years now."

"Well, I'll pass you on it this time but it's going to end," he said.

"Oh really, and why is that?" I asked. "Because it's dangerous. One of your tenants can run their hands down this thing and get a splinter from it."

"You've got to be kidding me" I laughed. "Do you want me to start passing out tweezers when we sign the lease?" He didn't think my joke was as funny as I did and I knew I was in for some fun with this guy!

Sure enough, about two weeks later, I received a call from Kevin, the head of inspections. I'll save you the 'he said' 'I said' part and just tell you that he put an end to the 2" × 4" railing trick. I told him that he was the one who originally passed and approved it. I also pleaded my case by asking him to put a grandfather rule in for railings. He was having none of it; the answer was 'no'! I guess after knocking on and passing the interior door, he had enough of my bullshit.

I knew I had to make the change but I still wanted to figure out a way to save face and a couple of bucks. I also wanted to jam it in the inspectors face, you know, kind of like you beat me but you didn't beat me. I came to the conclusion that if I entirely ripped down the 2" × 4"'s that were screwed to the wall, it would cost me some serious cash. Now I would not only be replacing them with railing, I would also have to purchase three railing brackets at about two bucks a piece. If I'm replacing two hundred railings, you can see where this starts to get expensive.

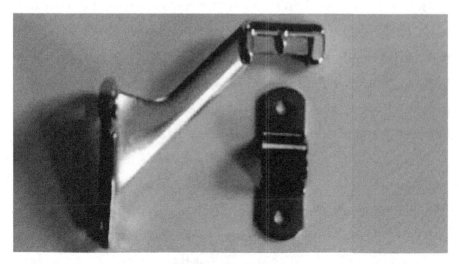

Railing brackets

What we did was simply leave the 2" × 4"'s in place and screwed the railing directly over top of it. Now when the tenant runs their hand down the railing, they won't be getting any poor little splinters. It saved time, cash and face!

When the inspector came back out to inspect the next house, he stood there staring at it. I could see he didn't like the way it was done and he wanted to fail me so bad but couldn't. He wanted a 'splinterless railing' and that's exactly what he got, without the brackets!

I don't know why I play these games with the inspectors. I guess it's a competitive thing. When they win, I lose cash. I don't like to lose at anything and I certainly don't like losing cash. So, yes, it pisses me off when somebody wants to change a rule in midstream. Tell me, did it really bother the inspector that I was using a 2" × 4" as a railing? Hell, no! It didn't bother the tenants either because they never challenged it. He was just going out of his way to break 'em for me. So just that little bit of satisfaction by doing it my way rather than his was worth its weight in gold. It was also worth its weight in cash because I saved about $1,200 by not having to purchase railing brackets! It's hard enough trying to keep up with tenant repairs; you don't need your inspectors trying to get into the act.

Final thoughts on rule changes – if you can't catch a break on a rule change by arguing, try to out think or out maneuver. If neither works, try threatening! Threatening usually works better when you own a lot of properties. For instance, if they wanted me to go back and start uncovering all of the windows that I have plywood and sided over, I wouldn't do it. I would threaten to terminate the lease and evict every single Section 8 tenant that I have on the program.

I would inform them that they had better get ready to do about two hundred more inspections and a ton of paperwork, not to mention about 1,000 calls from two hundred irate tenants, bitching and complaining that they now have to move.

Do everything you can do to turn the tables in your favor and come out on top! Don't let Section 8 push or boss you around. Without Section 8, you'll still survive by renting your houses out to private renters. Without us, the landlords, nobody down at Section 8 will survive. The tenants will be homeless or headed back to live in the projects, and the employees will be jobless and headed to the unemployment line. So every once in a while, let them know that they need you more than you need them!

CHAPTER 17

SHOP ON WHEELS

We added a new vehicle to our arsenal. We told you in Volume I how much time our stake body truck saved. Well, this vehicle saves even more time! Before I get into the details about this vehicle, let me tell you what drove us to get it.

About a year before we sold off our portfolio, we were really rocking and rolling. We were purchasing about six houses a month or more and getting them up and ready for move in. Our shop was 'state of the art' like a mini Home Depot. We had two crews going at it, seven days a week. We'd meet at the shop at 7:00 a.m., load up the trucks, and get the crews on their way.

It seemed as quick as the trucks rolled out, one would roll back in again. About ten minutes later, the other one would return. Nick or I would say, "Yo dude, you wrote a list of everything that you needed. What are you doing back here?" The answers never made any sense. The argument would sound something like this.

Worker – "I came back to get hinges for the door that I have to hang."

Nick – "You took the door, the doorknob, and the deadbolt, but you didn't take the hinges?"

Worker – "I had it written down on my list but I must have forgotten them."

Fine, everybody makes mistakes. Everybody forgets things once in a while. These guys, and I mean both crews, would each forget aboutthree things a day. Here's the kicker. When they came back to get a part, it wouldn't be just one of them in the truck. It would be two! We nipped that in the bud real fast. We told them only one guy comes back for parts. If two of you come back, two of you get fired! It's as simple as that.

By these guys coming back and forth all day, it was wasting time, gas, and manpower. We knew we had to do something fast before we lost our minds. Then we came up with a brilliant idea. Spartan!!!

Spartan truck

Many cabinets to hold materials in.

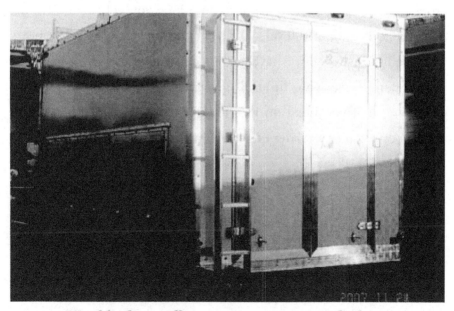

Double doors allow easy access to stock sheets of plywood and luan.

A Spartan is a truck that has more cabinets and bins on it than a custom kitchen. Also, the two back doors open and you can fit full sheets of plywood, drywall, paneling, etc. in it.

We stocked the truck with at least two of everything that we used in our houses. It worked like a charm. When the workers rolled out of the gate in the morning, they didn't return until quitting time! It saved manpower by keeping them at the job site and gas by them not driving back and forth all day. There would have been no way we would have been able to keep up with the turnovers without this vehicle.

We purchased a 2003 leftover in 2004. The sticker price on the truck was $30,000; we purchased the truck for $25,000. It was worth every cent. If you're just starting out and only own a couple of properties, this is not the truck for you. Once you get up around the thirty or forty property level, you might want to check into one of these vehicles. It doesn't have to be brand new. All it has to be is reliable and save you time. I guarantee you that if you have everything that you need on the truck that is parked out in front of the property you're working on, you'll save nothing but time!

CHAPTER 18

NEW PRODUCTS

Products change like the weather. One day you're turning a screw with a screwdriver, the next day you're using a screw gun. One day they're driving nails with a hammer, now everybody is using nail guns. Somebody is always going to come up with an easier way of doing something. That's just what new ideas do; they make your life easier. This is what I intend on doing for you in this chapter, make your life easier. I'll talk about a couple of new tools we have been using, some new products we switched over to, and I'll tell you a little bit about how we go shopping.

Make no mistake about it, Nick is the shopper! I'd rather stay at the jobsite rather than run from store to store, but Nick seems to enjoy it. Not only does he enjoy it, he's really good at it and saves us a lot of money. There are several different ways that he cuts costs and that's the first thing you'll be reading about.

How to shop – I'm sure that about 90% of you use Home Depot for your supplies. If you don't, you should. Their prices are lower than everybody else's and when you have to make a return, you never get a hassle. (No, I don't own Home Depot stock, thank you!) Now that I've got you in the correct store, I'm gonna tell you Nick's technique. About once every two months, Home Depot will run a sale in the paper or if you have a credit card through them, they'll notify you about it by mail. It's not a sale on this item or that item; it's a sale on the entire store! Most of the time, it's a 10% off everything in the store for twenty- four hours. A couple of times I have seen it 20% off. What Nick will do is write a list of everything that we need or are low on. Then he'll buy in bulk, and I mean BULK! Here's why.

Let's say you needed plywood and purchased ten sheets on the day of the sale. These sheets may last you a week or two but, odds are, you're going to run out before the next sale. Now you're back to purchasing plywood at the regular price. If you think 20% doesn't make a big difference, check it out for yourself.

Nick will order a bunk of ¾" plywood (100 sheets) in one shot. We know this is going to last us until the next sale. Now check out the savings:

$$100 \text{ sheets of plywood}$$
$$x \ \$20.00 \text{ per sheet}$$
$$= \$2,000.00$$
$$- 20\%$$
$$= \$1,600.00$$

You just saved $400 on plywood alone. That's like getting twenty sheets for free. Nick does it with luan, faucets, sinks, toilets, stick down tile, tools that we need, etc., all the big ticket items that add up fast at the cash register. He's not going to buy one hundred doorstops at a buck a piece to save twenty bucks; we'll get that kind of stuff any time. If we start adding in some kitchen cabinets and bathroom vanities, our order will usually reach around $10,000. Knock of 20% and you just save yourself two grand. Not bad for a day's work.

Here are two added bonuses. First, when you keep a good amount of stock, you don't have to keep running back and forth to the store, burning gas, wasting time, and standing in line. Who needs it? I think some guys live at Home Depot. Every time I go there I see the same guys and they all want to bullshit with me! Don't these guys want to finish what they are doing and get home? Well, perhaps not. But anyway, you get my point.

When I know I'm going to Home Depot to save a couple grand, I love it there. If I'm in the middle of a job and run out of say, Liquid Nails, I hate having to get back into my truck and make the unpleasant drive to Home Depot. Thanks to Nick, that rarely happens.

The second added bonus is free delivery! How can you beat that? We used to have to go into the store, pick out and load up everything that we wanted, wait in line, load the stock onto our trucks, drive back to the shop, then unload everything into the shop into its proper place. What a pain in the balls, literally!

Home Depot will deliver free if you spend over $400. The first couple of times they would get a couple of items wrong. Instead of a

2' × 4' ceiling tile, they might send us a 2' × 2' box of ceiling tile. Nick fixed that fast! What he did one day was go into Home Depot and wrote down the skew number to every product that we use. Now, when ordering, there are no mistakes. Instead of asking for a tub of 3" drywall screws, he'll just say "give me three tubs of A-234-633."

Home Depot is not the only company that runs sales like this so, needless to say, Nick shops in bulk at a couple of different stores. If MAB is running a special for buy one gallon of paint, get one free, Nick will purchase fifty gallons and get the next fifty free! Everything is done in bulk. I use to pass out when I saw him coming into the shop with 200 rolls of paper towels. Then I got used to it. He'd always say, "Mike, don't be cheap. We're gonna use it anyway so we might as well get it when it's on sale." He was right; now I shop the same way. You'll spend more in the long run by not buying in bulk and plus you'll never run out of anything!

Here is one more great thing about Home Depot (you gotta believe me, I have no ties to Home Depot, I just love their prices). Let's say you purchased the 100 sheets of plywood after sale price for $16 a sheet. Now let's say the price of plywood dips to $15 a sheet. Simply take back your receipt and they will refund you a hundred buck! ($1 for each sheet)

If you plan to shop this way, in bulk, call Home Depot and ask to speak to someone at the "Pro Desk." You'll be glad you did and so will your wallet!

CHAPTER 19

PRODUCT CHANGES

You're gonna love some of these, I guarantee it! Here is the first one. In Volume I, I told you to only paint with semi-gloss. Well, there has been a rule change. Don't get me wrong, the MAB semi-gloss is still a great product and holds up fine. In fact, I used it in the kitchen of my own home. Like I said in Volume I, if you see a smudge or dirt mark, wet a rag and simply wipe it off. Then what's the problem, you ask. Nothing is wrong with the paint. It's the tenants! They don't wipe anything off!

I finally started to figure, "Why the hell am I paying $10 more for a five-gallon bucket of semi-gloss...When I could just use the cheaper flat paint?" I pay $40 for a five-gallon bucket of semi-gloss and $30 for a five of flat. Ninety percent of the tenants aren't going to wipe anything down. They would rather call you 25 times to ask you when you're coming out to repaint the house. One lady thought we would be out once a year. What a joke!

We no longer use semi-gloss.

Even though I knew they weren't wiping down the walls, I continued to purchase the semi-gloss and take the $10 hit. Not because I felt that the tenants would change their ways, but because if somebody moved out, it was easier to repaint the house with what was already on the walls because it covers easier.

What did I switch to and why? Let me give you the why first. By accident, that's why! What happened is we purchased a house that had one of those funky colored living rooms. It was almost like a lima bean green. In fact, I was waiting for the Jolly Green Giant to jump out at me from behind the dining room wall. Anyway, they had crazy colors throughout the house.

I asked the painter for his material list and he told me he would need 3, five gallon buckets of semi-gloss and 3, five gallon buckets of primer. A primer is something that you put on the walls before the semi- gloss so that the crazy colors don't bleed through. The semi-gloss I had in stock, the primer I did not. I proceeded to MAB to get the primer. Of course, I asked for the cheapest primer in stock. What they gave me was "Pro-30 Primer" which went for $18 a five. I picked up 3 five gallon buckets totaling $54 and was on my way. I dropped off the supplies to the painter and was on my way to chase after another adventure.

The next morning, I arrive at the property before the painter to check on his progress. I not only wanted to see what got done, I also wanted to see if the primer was covering. Man oh man, was it ever! The walls looked terrific. They looked like they were rolled out in MAB's most expensive flat paint.

When the painter arrived he said, "It looks like the primer worked; the walls are ready for the semi-gloss."

I said, "They shit, I'm leaving them just like this!"

"What are you going to do with the semi-gloss you bought?" he asked. I told him that I'm returning it. Not only did I return those 3 fives, I returned every one of them that we had in stock! Now, I'm getting paint on the walls at less than half price. Section 8 tenants don't know it's primer, Section 8 inspectors don't know it's primer, but I do. I also know how much I'm saving!

Another thing that I do now is purchase the one gallon empty tins that they sell at MAB.

Tins used to hold touch-up paint.

They cost about $2. Then I fill the tin with a gallon of primer and hand it to the tenant when they move in. I tell them that we don't come out to repaint the property, so here is a gallon of paint that you can use for touch-ups. It keeps me from having to pick up the phone and hear, "Mr. Mike, when are you coming back out to repaint my house?"

Rule Change – only paint with "Pro 30 Primer"
Product Change – switched from $40 semi-gloss to $18 primer

Plywood – for years we had been using the good (expensive) plywood. I just figured that if I was closing off an enclosed porch or a couple of basement windows with it, I might as well use the good stuff. I didn't want to come back in two years and find the plywood rotting away.

This past summer (2007), we hired an out-of-work union carpenter. There was an enclosed porch with nine windows on it that

I wanted plywood and sided over. When he pulled his truck into the shop to load up the materials, he asked, "What the hell are you using this shit for?"

"Enlighten me, what should I be using?" I asked.

He knew right away that the 1/2" plywood we were using cost $15 per sheet. "Mike, use the OSB 5/8" plywood. It only costs $10 per sheet and all you're doing is covering over windows with it."

I asked, "Yeah, but won't it eventually rot out?" "Hell, no! That's all they're using in new construction these days and you don't see any new houses falling down do you? You'll be long gone or dead by the time this wood rots out."

It doesn't take much for me to be talked into saving a buck! I switched from $15 per sheet of plywood to $10 a sheet so fast it would make your head spin. His idea made sense. He had the right answers, 23 years of experience, and I love saving cash. It was a great idea and OSB is even a little thicker than the regular plywood. I can't understand why people are frightened of change or new ideas. Hell, I'm frightened of the old ones!

Product Change -$15 per sheet plywood to $10 per sheet plywood

We switched from this plywood …

… to this plywood

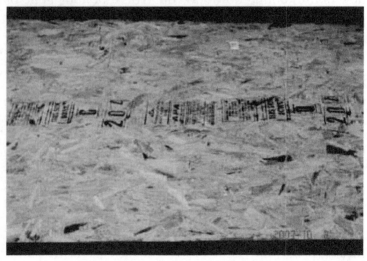

Vinyl patch –

This is a product that we have been using for years and, boy is it a life saver! It's also a big money saver. Every so often we would get an inspector that wanted to break balls over a couple of spider web cracks on the sidewalk. The cracks weren't bad enough for you to trip over but something had to be done. We didn't want to rip out and replace the entire block, yet on the other hand, if nothing were done, we would fail the inspection.

The answer was Vinyl Patch! It mixes easy with water, has no stones in it so it goes on smooth, and will certainly get you through your inspection.

We don't even take any chances anymore. When we are getting the property ready for inspection, we fill in every single crack on the sidewalk. You don't need an inspector failing you for something as asinine as a small crack on a cement block.

MICHAEL MCLEAN & NICK CIPRIANO

You can find this product at Home Depot and it costs $9 a bag. It will save you from replacing countless sidewalk blocks at $150 per block.

Product – vinyl patch

Price -$9 per bag

Tools – I won't get too carried away here talking about tools. First of all, I could talk about them all day and second of all, most likely nobody would switch from what they are using to what I'm using. Tools cost money so if I said I only use a Dewalt 18-volt screw gun, are you going to throw your Makita screw gun away and run out and get a Dewalt? No, of course not. (For those of you who answered yes, I now have you brainwashed. Please send all your money and valuable to P.O. Box 479, Folcroft, PA)

That's why the two tools I'm going to recommend you get are inexpensive. For $7 or $30.00, you might want to give them a shot and see if they are as good as I say.

First tool – Husky Razor Knife – cost $7.50

A real time saver

Over the past twenty years, I have put down a thousand stick down tile floors. For years, I used the old type of utility knife.

A real headache to change blades.

They worked terrific but were such a pain in the ass to change the blades on. You needed a screwdriver, then you had to line the blade and the dispenser up to put it back together. Then if you were off by just a little bit, you would have to take the thing apart again. Some of them even had the little spring inside which really took a long time to get back together. You hate like hell to get rolling on a floor and then have to stop and change a blade. Half of the time I would finish the floor with a blade that was as sharp as a butter knife just so I wouldn't have to stop.

Now it's no longer a problem! Husky has come out with a razor knife that is awesome! You can change a blade out in about 20 seconds. You no longer need a screwdriver and you don't have to line a damn thing up. When the knife is open, it has a safety feature that locks the blade in place. The knife even comes with a mounted clip so you can attach it to your belt or pocket. This knife is very slick and a real time saver.

Second tool – Jet Swet – cost $30.00

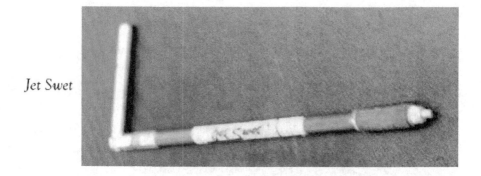

Jet Swet

Cutting out as many hose bibs and washing machine hook-ups as I have, I don't know how I ever lived without this tool! It's clever, easy to use, and will save you a ton of time. Have you ever been in the basement of your home and had to replace a shut off valve but you couldn't get the back flow of water to stop trickling through the valve long enough to solder it? You probably tried the old tricks like stuffing a piece of bread into the line or tilting the line upward to cut off the flow of water. It never really works and you end up rattling off about a hundred of the foulest curse words in the book. Shortly after that you throw down your torch and decide to just wait an hour for the entire house to drain down, which not only takes time but also leaves you with a soaking wet basement floor.

Now, it's no longer a problem! Jet Swet has come up with the greatest plumbing invention since PVC. What you do is simply insert the one end into your 1/2" line, tighten the nut on the back which expands the rubber and cuts the back flow of water entirely. Now, just sweat on your new shut off valve, remove your Jet Swet, and call it a day. No more cursing or waiting. They sell these things in all different sizes, however, I have only had to use the 1/2" and ¾" ones. I have included some directions and a pricing chart on this tool. I know I say that a 1/2" Jet Swet cost $30 and they say $42.00, but I purchased mine at my local plumbing supply house for thirty bucks and I'm sure you can do the same.

CHAPTER 20

FINDING HOUSES

"How and where did you find all those houses?" I was asked this question so many times that I had to write a chapter about it. I was asked not only by landlords and people who have read the book, but also by family members and acquaintances. Although the answer is 'it really wasn't that hard', many people still don't believe it. If you want something bad enough, you're going to get it or die trying! Also, you have to stick to your guns and make sure you don't overpay. Those are the only things that you have to get into your mind when you set out to build an empire. Determination and common sense -with those two things in your corner, nothing can stop you!

When we were at the height of our purchasing run, the appraised value of a home was about 50k for a house in Southwest Philadelphia. That's about how much a typical finished home would go for. That's great, if you're selling a home! Unfortunately, we are in the business of purchasing homes. What's the difference? Well, when you're selling a home and you hear that most of the people in the neighborhood are getting 60k, you want to get it too. Now, if you're buying a home, you want to get it for less than 60k.... way less! If you heard about a home on the street that sold for 15k five years ago, that's what you want to get yours for.

It is in this area where fortunes are made or lost. Some people who think they want to be the next Donald Trump start playing with scared money. They get offered a good deal on a home and still try to underbid it. The next thing you know, they lose the deal and end with nothing. They don't wise up and they end up losing more homes than they end up getting. I'm not saying you can't give a guy a ridiculous offer just to find out where a seller's bottom is; but once you know you've hit it, you'd better jump on the deal if the numbers work.

Then there is the other side of the coin. Some people want to get into the real estate game so bad and quickly that they end up overpaying. I've seen guys come along in our neighborhood and overpay for a house that is under 60k. How can they be overpaying for a house if they get it under 60k you ask? Easy, follow along!

There are a lot of hidden costs when buying a house and you must take them all into consideration. Although it sounds complicated, it's really not. Here is an example. Okay, you pick up the house for 52k, eight grand less than what the neighborhood appraises out at. Let's say your closing costs are three grand and insurance costs you another five hundred bucks. You now have $55,500 invested before you even open the door.

You start to rehab the property and end up sinking in another $5,800. You're now at $61,300 and already $1,300 over the appraised value. Now, if you want to sell it, you would need to get about 66k just to break even and get your investment of $61,300 back. I say 66k because you would have to pay realtor fees and closing fees to sell the house also. That is about $4,700 bucks more than anybody else is getting on the block. It is also the type of deal that Nick and I would thumb our noses at and say, "Next!"

Nick and I made a living on excellent deals, deals that made sense. What's a deal that makes sense? One you can't lose a nickel on! How did we get them? By having the balls to look at a guy who was selling a house for $60k directly in the face and saying, "I'll give you $25k."

More often than not, they would ask, "Are you kidding me?" Or scream, "I'm insulted!" Yeah, like I care about insulting a seller. Here is a guy who is trying to get out of the city. He's got a house that he hasn't put a nickel into in twenty years, yet he thinks that since everyone else on the block is getting 60k that he should get it too. Sorry, it doesn't work that way. I'm the one that should be insulted.....insulted because this guy thinks I'm blind or a fool.

We'd always leave it like this. "Listen buddy, we're not out here trying to insult anybody. To us, it's just business. If you change your mind or want to hit us with a counter offer, here is our card." The real desperate (dumb) ones usually wouldn't let you make it to the door before they threw another offer at you. Now, we know we've got 'em!

"Can you give me $40K?" Wow, that was hard! I'm in the house for five minutes and the price just dropped 33%. "Nah, it's not worth forty to me. But what I will do is pay cash, no inspections, and I'll have you out of here in thirty days or less." I'd say our success rate was about 45% in getting the deals. The other 55% we were going to end up overpaying for and that wasn't going to happen. If we were baseball players, Nick and I would both be in the Hall of Fame with that kind of average! Also, we were looking at about thirty houses a month so you can see how our volume of houses skyrocketed quickly.

Here is the formula that we invented and stuck to. It's a formula that will work every time and, if you don't bend or waiver, it will work for you also.

#1. Naturally, you want to continue to pull money out of one house to purchase the next. For Nick and I, that wasn't good enough. Not only did we want to pull money out of the home to buy the next, we also wanted to line our pockets with a couple of grand!

#2. You want to find the bank that's going to give you the highest LTV (loan to value) at the lowest rate. It might take a day of shopping, but you will eventually find it.

#3. You want to get the deal in place at the lowest possible price that you can get. What the seller sets the asking price at should be of no concern to you. What you're going to or can pay for the house is the only thing you have to worry about.

Let's say the bank that you chose is going to give you an 80% LTV loan. That means if the appraised value comes back at $60k, you can borrow up to $48k from the bank (80% of $60,000 = $48,000.00). What you have to do is keep the price of the house, the closing costs, and the repairs as much under the $48,000 as possible. Remember, forget completely about what the seller is asking for the house; that number means absolutely nothing to you. The closing costs on a house that sells for between $20k and $50k are going to be in the ballpark of $4k.

#4. Now, you have to figure out what your repairs will cost. When looking at a house, check the majors (heat, hot water heater, roof, electric service, windows, bathroom, and kitchen). Your mind should start to work like a calculator. Early on, you might actually need to bring a pen, paper and calculator with you but the more houses you look at, you'll see how easy it gets!

If the property needs a new heater, write down $2,000 on your paper. If it needs a rubber roof, write down $900. If it needs nine windows, write down $1,350 (9 × $150 per window). These prices are all examples; they are what I pay my contractors to get these jobs done. You should know exactly what you will be paying for repairs such as these. Anyway, now add up your total repairs. Let's say they total $6,000. Take the $6,000 in repairs and add it to you $4,000 closing costs.

Total repairs	$ 6,000.00
Closing costs	$ 4,000.00
	$10,000.00

#6. Now minus this number from the maximum LTV (loan to value) that you can borrow on a $60,000 appraisal. Our LTV was 80% ($48,000.00).

Maximum amount you can borrow	$48,000.00
Minus total closing and repair costs	$10,000.00
	$38,000.00

You now know that the maximum you will be able to pay in this deal is $38,000. You will be able to purchase the home ($38,000), pay your closing costs ($4,000) and complete your repairs ($6,000), all of which will total $48,000. If you pay more for the property, you'll be taking money out of your pocket. Every dollar less than the $38,000 will go directly into your pocket!

#7. Go to the bank and take the loan for $48,000. Now, you've got every cent of your money back and you're ready to hunt down the next deal! Also, you have added another property to your portfolio that has positive cash flow. The typical payment for a $48,000 loan at 6% for 20 years is $343. The rent that you receive on a 3-bedroom row home in Philadelphia is $800.

$$\begin{array}{r} \$800.00 \text{ Rent Received} \\ -\$343.00 \text{ Loan Payment} \\ \hline \$457.00 \text{ Positive Cash Flow} \end{array}$$

#8. Get shrewd! I said breaking even was never good enough for Nick and I, nor should it be for you. In a deal like the one I described above, we would have offered the home owner about $28,000 and stuck the extra $10,000 in our pockets.

Never be afraid or embarrassed to lowball. If you don't get the deal, so what, more will follow. Also, you'll probably never see the guy again in your life so who cares what he thinks of you. If the shoe were on the other foot, believe me, the homeowner would do the same to you. I'll give you two more quick stories about trying to hammer out a price on a property – one, I felt great after, the other I wanted to throw up after!

First story – the good one. There was an old factory in the neighborhood which we invest in. We had never seen anybody coming or going in or out of it. Finally, a 'For Sale' sign ended up on it. Commercial buildings are not really our cup of tea, so we never pursued it. After the property sat for about a year, curiosity had gotten the best of me. I ran into the realtor that had the property for sale. I knew the realtor very well from purchasing homes from him.

"Hey, Bill, what's that guy asking on that warehouse over on 71st Street?"

He answered $180,000.

"Why, do you want to take a look at it?"

"Sure."

We met at the property. I took a quick look around and said, "Offer him $60k cash with no inspections and a thirty-day closing."

"Mike, I can't call him with that offer, he'll laugh me off the phone."

"Yeah, that's okay; maybe we'll all get a good laugh. Call him!"

"Mike, really I can't. I'd only be wasting his time and yours."

"Okay Bill, I'm gonna call him myself. I'll find out who owns the building and just do it myself." I said.

From selling us properties in the past, this guy knew I would do exactly what I said. I don't throw around false threats. I make a lot of threats, mainly to tenants but, believe me, if things don't go my way, the threats become promises. Besides, he wasn't wasting anyone's time. What would it take to make a phone call.... two minutes? He just didn't want to make the offer because he was afraid the seller would take it, and that would lower the realtor's commission dramatically. Now, if I called the seller giving him the offer, and he accepted, the realtor wouldn't get a cent....especially if I told the seller that his realtor didn't want to bring him 'such a low offer'.

Anyway, Bill called the guy and he says, "No way!" No sweat off my ass. I really didn't need the property anyway. However, about two months go by and my phone rings.

"Mike, it's Bill. Listen, are you still interested in that warehouse for $60k?" Although I was and my ears stood straight up when I thought I was going the steal this property at $60k.

I said, "Nah, that ship sailed about two months ago. Tell him I'll give him $50k." Guess what, he took it!

Nick and I cleaned the property out, painted it, and sold it 26 days later for $155,000. Maybe if the owner would have taken the four days that it took us to clean out the property and paint it, he would have received the same. Instead, he was lazy and ended up losing a nice piece of change. *Opportunity is missed by most people because it is disguised in overalls and looks like work.* (Thomas Edison)

Now for the bad story. Believe it or not, this mistake has happened to me a few times. I know, I know, I told you in Volume I that if you make a mistake, never let it come back to bite you in the ass again. There are exceptions to the rule. Sometimes you never know how low someone is willing to go. The only way to find out is by making an offer.

We were pretty new at the game and went over to take a look at a 'for sale by owner' property. An older Italian woman owned the house and it was as clean as a whistle. Upgrades galore, beautiful kitchen, ceramic bathroom and you could eat off the floors! Right from the get go she was complaining about the neighborhood....loud music, dogs barking, her neighbor parks in front of her house, everyone she knew for years moved out, yadda, yadda, yadda. I could already feel my adrenaline rising. This lady was talking way too much. Buying and selling properties is like a game of poker. Keep a straight face, say nothing positive or negative, and you'll always come out a lot better off! I think that by the time I was ready to make her an offer, I knew how many cars the neighbors owned and what the mileage was on them.

Anyway, I knew I had her and I went in for the kill. Not that I would take advantage of an old lady or anything like that but, okay, you're right, I would! "How much are you asking?" I asked.

"Forty thousand" she replied.

"I'll give you $25k."

"Fine" she said, "Sold!"

I was waiting for a counter offer that never came. Even though it was a terrific deal at $25,000 for a house that didn't need a damn thing, I was sick! If I would have said $15k, would she have sold? I'll never know.

I do know that I didn't get any sleep that night and for the next three weeks leading up to the settlement, I drove poor Nick crazy. "What do you think she would have gone for?"

"What do you think was her bottom line?"

"I wonder if she would have taken $10K?" Finally, he had had enough of my 'what ifs.'

"Mike, just let it go. It's over and done with."

Well, the only way for me not to think about money is to have a great deal of it, and I ain't there yet!

Then Nick said something that is totally true. He said, "You can always come up on your offer but you can never, ever go back down." I wanted to ask the woman after settlement (just for the hell of it) what she would have taken for the house. Then I said to myself, don't get yourself sick again. If she would have said five grands, I don't think that I would have slept for a month!

Before you open your mouth and throw that first offer out there, remember, the number you first give out is the very least you will be paying for the property. So think about that before making any offers. A slip of the foot you may soon recover but a slip of the tongue you may never get over!

That is the 'how' we were able to afford so many properties. Now, I'll tell you how we found the properties and, believe me, it wasn't rocket science!

It was 1997 when Nick and I jumped into the Section 8 game. The neighborhood (Southwest Philadelphia) was just starting to change. A lot of the big businesses were either closing down or relocating. People who had lived in the neighborhood for years, now wanted to get out. What worked out great was that there were thousands of people who wanted to sell and not a lot of people who were willing to buy. Nick and I were two of those people who were ready, willing, and able to buy and we let it be known!

First, we had cards printed up that simply said, "We Buy Houses." We went into every single real estate office in South and Southwest Philly and handed out the cards. The calls started to come in immediately. Our three big advantages were number 1, we pay cash, number 2, there would be no inspections by a home or city inspector before purchasing and number 3, we will get the deal done in 30 days or less. We wanted the property fast; they wanted to get out even faster.

Word started to spread between the South and Southwest Philly realtors that these two guys wanted to buy! They don't play games, they come in with cash and they get the deal done. We were a realtor's dream.

Our business card

Another thing we did, which most of the realtors didn't like, was give the sellers our card and tell them that if they knew anybody else that wanted to sell to give us a call. We told the seller that if they recommended us and we closed a deal because of their lead, we would give them $300 bucks. The reason the realtors didn't like it is because they weren't getting the leads nor were they willing to pay for them like we did. It didn't stop the realtors from calling us though. They like money just as much as the next guy.

Soon we had homeowners and realtors calling us seven days a week. We looked at every single property that we were called about....didn't miss one! Our portfolio began to grow and grow. We also ran an ad in the city paper. This ad simply said, "We Buy Houses for Cash and Fast!" It was a 3" × 3" ad that, to be honest, we weren't getting a lot of calls from. Then we changed the ad to color. Boy, what a difference! It was like night and day. For the extra $50 bucks, our phone was ringing off the hook!

Then Nick came up with a great idea, although I didn't like it at first. "Let's run the whole back page of the paper."

"What, are you crazy?" I said. "That's gonna cost about $500 bucks!"

"Seven hundred....I already checked" Nick said. "Mike, think about it. If we get one good deal a month from that ad, one where we stick about $15k into our pockets, the ad will have paid for itself thirty times over."

When I thought about it like that, I couldn't agree more. We ran the ad!

The phone never stopped ringing and we never stopped wheeling and dealing. We loved it! I remember one time a guy worked split shift. His first shift was 10:00 p.m. until 3:00 a.m. Then he went back in from 6:00 a.m. until 11:00 a.m. He told us we couldn't look at the house during the day because he went home and would go directly to bed. We looked at the house at 3:30 a.m. between his split shift! By 4:30 a.m. we had an agreement of sale signed.

If we were to say how we picked off most of our homes, I would say it was through word of mouth. If we purchased a house from someone on the 6500 block of Wheeler Street, within a month someone else from Wheeler Street would be calling and asking, "You bought the Sweeney's house....can you buy mine?" It actually got to be funny on a street named Theodore. I think we owned twelve homes on this block and thought we'd soon own the entire block.

The 6500 block of Theodore St.

Nick and I owned every home that you are looking at.

The reason word of mouth spread so quickly is because we were straight shooters. Although we always came in with a low offer, we got the deal done. We never screwed anybody or left anybody holding their hand on their ass at the settlement table. We wanted to get the deal done worse than they wanted to sell their house. You just can't let them know that. And don't feel sorry for the sellers; we didn't put a gun to their heads and make them sign a low offer agreement. If they could have received more, they would have had someone else buy their house.

Anyway, finding ways to get good deals is almost like 'eliminating.' You've got to think of new ideas and new angles to get what you want. You'll try some things where your phone may not ring at all. Then you'll try something else and it will ring off the hook. It's all about being inventive......the more inventive you get, the more your phone will ring!

Sometimes, imagination is more important than knowledge.
(Ben Franklin)

CHAPTER 21

RENT INCREASES

Every year, Section 8 will send you out a "Rent Increase" form. Not that they want to increase your rent; it's because they have to send you out the form. It's the law that they have to send you out the form, but here is the catch. Just because they send it to you and you fill it out and send it back, it doesn't mean that they have to approve your "Rent Increase Request." They can simply just say your request has been denied.

Now, there are several things that you can do. The first would be to do nothing and wait until next year. Next year will roll around again and history will repeat itself. Again you will be denied and perhaps the following year you won't even bother filling out the damn form. This is exactly what Section 8 wants you to do – give up! You end up playing right into their hands.

Soon, five years go by and you have not seen one rent increase. Now, homes on the street are renting for $750 and you're still stuck at $625. What you're doing is losing $1,500 per year just by being lazy;

$1,500 in Philly is enough to pay the taxes and insurance for the year! Here are a couple of things that we have done.

The minute I get done filling out a "Rent Increase Form," I get into my truck and drive it, not mail it, back down to the Section 8 office! The name of the tenant's Service Rep will be right on the form. When I go into the office, she is the person that I want to speak to. If they tell you that she's busy, tell them that you'll wait. If the entire ordeal takes 3 hours and you get your raise, that comes out to $500 an hour! It's worth the wait.

Another thing that it does is show the Service Rep that you care about getting this rent increase. She probably sits at her desk opening envelopes and stamping "Denied" on every one of them....but yours will be different. It'll be hand-delivered and, it never hurts to throw in a request (or lie) such as, "I just installed new windows in this house and I need to get that rent increase." Most of these Service Reps never call the tenants to check if you did any upgrades at the property and, if they did check, you could always say, "Oh, I must have gotten that house mixed up with another one of my rentals." Don't you love this book; I even show you how to lie!

Lying to Service Reps and tenants is like second nature to me. When I tell you I am a stand-up guy, I truly am! I don't have to lie in my real life because I'm never out to screw anybody or take money out of their pockets. My landlord life, that's a different story. It seems all tenants and Section 8 try to do is screw you out of money and I'm gonna lie, cheat, and fight not to get more, but to get what is rightfully mine and what I feel I deserve. It's kind of like the innocent guy who goes to jail and says, "I didn't learn how to be a crook until I ended up in here."

Anyway, back to the rent increases. Don't get crazy and ask for five or six percent because you're not going to get it. Ask for about three percent and there is a good chance you'll get it. On a $700 rent, you'll receive a $21 per month increase....not bad! At that rate, you should be able to keep your rates average with everyone else's rents as the years roll by.

Now, let's say for some reason you get denied. The first thing I do is get back in my truck and head back down to speak to the Service Rep again. A piece of paper stamped "Denied" is not good enough for me! If she denied it, I want to know why. If she says that would be too high of a rent increase, I come right out and say, "Let's negotiate.... what do you think is fair because I'm not leaving here with nothing" Usually, I'll end up with a two or two and a half percent rent increase which is fine; at least the rent went up. You've got to pick your battles in life but I believe whenever I am due a rent increase, there's gonna be a battle!

Okay, you end up with a Service Rep who isn't willing to give you a nickel rent raise. She thinks she's the accountant for Section 8. The first thing I always ask her is if she got a raise this year. That's just me being a smart ass; that won't help you. The second thing that I do that will help you is to write your tenant a letter saying you will not be renewing his or her lease (again, we put it in our lease that if we are denied a yearly rent increase, we have the option to terminate the lease in 30 days).

When the tenant receives this letter, they usually hit the roof and that is exactly what you want them to do. We simply tell them that, "Hey, I want to keep you but Section 8 doesn't want to increase the rent and, according to our lease, we can legally do this. We can get more money renting the property to a private renter and, as much as we hate to lose a good tenant like you, this is a business and we are in it for the money."

Even if you have no intention of getting rid of the tenant if the Service Rep doesn't increase the rent, still play the game because you have nothing to lose. The worst you can do is leave your tenant in place with the same rent. Anyway, tell the tenant to call her Service Rep and let the Rep know that they don't want to leave. I've done this many times and it has worked like a charm! The Service Rep will call you back and ask, "Will you take a 2% increase?" Take it, keep the tenant, and get ready for next year's battle.

I am no fool and I know as much as the Service Rep loved telling me, "Sorry Mr. Landlord, no raise," they hate like hell telling the tenant to find a new place to live. After all, these are people they are supposed to be watching out for and representing. When they have a tenant telling them they can't afford a moving truck, they have no money for another security deposit, and they love the home they're in, watch how fast the Service Reps cave in! The $21 raise that I wanted meant nothing to the Service Rep; there was no money to be found. When a tenant calls and says they can't afford a moving truck, money appears out of thin air.

I'll never ever stop fighting for money that belongs to me or should be coming my way. Once you give up that fight, you might as well sell off your properties because there is nothing left to fight for!

I'm going to tell one more crazy, funny story and then I'll put an end to this chapter. We purchased a property off a guy who had been renting the property to a Section 8 tenant for the past six years. I think I've only purchased two or three properties with tenants already in them and this was one of those times. Anyway, I had owned several properties on the block and had been getting $725 rent for a three bedroom, which this property was. However, the guy I bought the property from hadn't received a rent increase in six years; his rent hadn't changed from the original rent that he received and it was stuck at $550.00.

Well, when rent increase time rolled around, I asked for 5% and was denied. I told the Service Rep that I just rented a property on this block to a Section 8 tenant and was granted a rent of $725. She wasn't having any of it and still said 'no'. To make a long story short, I didn't renew the tenant's lease and they vacated the property. We painted, cleaned, and re-rented the property for $725 to guess who? You got it, the tenant that we had just told to move! She was staying at her mother's house while she looked for a new place to live and saw our house listed for rent. Well, she just loved what we did to the joint and the best part was that she didn't even have to change her address on her license.

How stupid is Section 8 sometimes? Man, you've just got to scratch your head and say, "What a pack of idiots!" Here is this Service Rep breaking my balls like she is trying to save the government a ton of cash. If she would have just given me the 5% increase like I had asked for, that would have brought the rent up to $577. Instead, she ends up costing them $148 bucks a month!

CHAPTER 22

EVICTIONS

I'll keep this short and not so sweet because, God knows, I could go on and on about this subject forever! "Eviction" is a word no landlord ever wants to hear. How tenants ever had the rules turned in their favor is beyond me. It's the biggest injustice in business and it makes me sick that you have to spend money, after losing money, to get some low life out of your house.

Every time I go to court, it's the same bullshit! Whether it's my tenant pulling it or the eviction cases heard before mine, it's always the same. The landlord says the tenant is three months behind on the rent and then the tenant says, "I wasn't paying the rent because he wasn't fixing things in the property. He's a slumlord."

Right then and there, the judge should have the balls and common sense to say, "Get out of my courtroom, you bum." Why? That's easy to answer. First of all, if you were living in a house that everything was broken and nobody was fixing it, would you want to go to court and fight to stay there? Hell, no! The landlord wouldn't have to ask me to leave; I'd go on my own.

Secondly, why don't the judges ever ask, "Well, how did all those things in the property get broken?" I've lived in my house for the past nine years and I've never had a bedroom door suddenly fall off the hinges. No fist-sized holes suddenly appear in my drywall. The handles and knobs to my faucets, tub, and stove always stayed intact and never disappeared.

This was the kind of bullshit that tenants would try to win a court battle with. I also loved it when they would bring pictures to court of a property that they demolished as proof. They'd take pictures of filthy carpets or a hole in the ceiling from where they overflowed the toilet. I swear to you, even if it wasn't my case being heard, it would get Nick and I so mad that on several occasions we spoke up and had to be escorted out of the courtroom. That's right, they'd make us wait out in the hallway until it was our turn in "Romper Room" ......that's what we call the courtroom!

What gets you pissed is the judge is sitting there looking at the pictures in disbelief like, "Your poor tenant, you!" This is supposed to be a man or woman who is 'educated'. It shouldn't take an education to realize that the tenant didn't rent the property in that type of condition so any damage must have been done by them! And the pictures? Now they're just bringing in more evidence to hang themselves with as far as I'm concerned.

I promise you, this is a true story. We were in court and a tenant brought in about ten pictures of damages and also twenty liars (witnesses). As we were waiting for our case to be heard, we were watching this poor landlord take an hour and a half ass whipping from the judge, the tenant, and all twenty witnesses. Yes, the judge heard every witness the tenant brought with her! Only three of them were even on the lease. Here is the kicker. The pictures of the damages were blown up to 8" × 12"s. Not only did the judge look at them in awe, she held them up so the entire courtroom could view them! I could have sworn that I was in "Judge Judy's" courtroom.

It seemed as though the judge wanted some class participation so Nick and I decided to play along. After all, if the judge was being this rotten to a sixty-year-old landlord who came to court in a suit, it was only going to get worse for two 38-year-old guys who weren't wearing suits. I was so mad that this judge was wasting an hour and a half of my time and so sick of the piece of shit tenant calling the landlord a 'slumlord' that I spoke up when the next picture was put on display. It was a picture of the dirtiest carpet you had ever seen; if I owned a pet rat, I wouldn't let him walk across it. Once again, the judge held the picture up so all could see and the tenant, once again, chimed in with, "I told you he was a slumlord." I yelled up to the front of the courtroom, "By the looks of that carpet, I'd say you're a slum tenant!" I was the first to be shown where the exit sign was. Nick was a close second when he asked the judge if this was a murder trial or an eviction. Why so many witnesses and why was this damn thing taking all day? He soon joined me out in the hallway.

Anyway, here is my point. You don't want to let your beef with your tenant get as far as the courtroom. The best way to do this is to insulate yourself with a great lease. In it, you want the tenant to sign every form and piece of paper that says they are responsible for everything and you are responsible for nothing. A great lease is something that you need more than anything else in this business.

Nick and I go above and beyond leases; we add addendums! The lease says it all and the addendums say it a second time in simple understandable English. If your tenant breaks a window and calls you to fix it, they might not understand or be able to find page 6, article 12, paragraph 9 which states, "As our tenant, you agree to be responsible for any items in the household which become broken by fault or no fault of yours." You'll probably get, "That don't mean I got to fix your window."

With addendums, your tenant has no fight whatsoever! Here is how our "Broken Window Addendum" reads:

BROKEN WINDOW ADDENDUM

I _____, the tenant residing at _____, take full responsibility for all windows in the property. I understand and agree that if any windows during my occupancy become broken, cracked or damaged in any way, I will take full responsibility in having them repaired at my own expense and none of these expenses will be reimbursed by the owner of the property. Whether by passer-by, act of nature, burglary or any other reason, I agree I can, will and should be evicted if the broken window in question is not repaired within 24 hours of being broken.

Tenant _____

Landlord _____

Now, when you make it that clear to the tenant, they have a choice to make. Do they go to court and try to lie their way out of this or do they fix the window? Ninety-nine percent will fix the window and the 1% that take you to court will lose. Even as dumb as half of these judges are, you've got a legalized document with your tenant's signature on it saying they are responsible for all broken windows. You didn't hold a gun to their heads when they signed it and, as bad as the "pro-tenant" judge wants to rule in the tenant's favor, they can't.

The lease and addendums are always great for threatening too! What we'll do is put a paragraph in the lease that says if any of the addendums are not followed or broken and leads to eviction; the tenant's voucher privileges will be revoked. I will guarantee you that 100% of the tenants will sign the lease without even reading it over. You know how many houses I have rented and I'll bet maybe only a handful even skimmed over the lease or asked a question before signing it. I'll also guarantee you this, first when you show them the 'Broken Window Addendum' that they signed, they'll more than likely fix the window. Second, if they give you any bullshit, point out the page in the lease that they also signed that puts their voucher privileges in harm's way and I guarantee you they won't be in a hurry to drag you into court for "not fixing anything."

Land lording is an easy game if played correctly and, when your opponent (the tenant) doesn't even bother to read the rules to the game (the lease), it makes it a whole lot easier to win the game!

Final note – In the beginning of Volume I, I came right out and told you that I am not trying to sell leases, products, CD's or seminars. What changed? Well, it seems that everybody and their brother want to purchase a copy of our lease! I love making a buck as much as the next guy, but there is a twist.

Our lease and addendums were written by three people......Nick, myself and, you guessed it, an attorney. The attorney, who did nothing except legalize the documents, wants to put a ridiculous price of $129 on the lease and take 70% of all sales. This is a guy who didn't write one clause, one paragraph, or one addendum. They only thing he had the power to do was get the lease approved as a legalized document. Now, he's like one of those pit bulls that bit the mailman in the ass and won't let go; unfortunately, his teeth are in my ass! The case is in Philadelphia court right now and who knows how long it will take to be heard let alone settled. We are in the process of trying to buy him out of his third interest in the lease but this ambulance chaser thinks that he deserves more (yes, Joel, I hope you read this!).

Anyway, for all of you that have asked, I promise you, the minute Nick and I get this worked out, I will make the lease and addendums available. It truly is a great lease that will not only protect you; it will keep you out of "Romper Room" as well!

CHAPTER 23

AFTER THE SELL OFF

Thousands and thousands of people who read the book wanted to know what Nick and I have been doing after the sell off all of our properties. I love a success story as much as anybody and I'd love to tell you that we retired. I'm sure that's what every single person who purchases this book has in mind or sets as a goal. Buy some properties, buy some more properties, real estate prices go crazy, you sell off your portfolio for an unbelievable profit and reap the rewards!

Honestly, we could have done just that. But really, we're both only forty years-old and still crave a good deal today as much as we did when we first got into this game. It's contagious, addicting, and I love it! I love every minute of it, from the time the phone rings to go check out a property, haggling back and forth over the price, and finally getting to the settlement table to close the deal.

It's like a professional athlete that has already made his money, hits forty years-old, and still continues to play. When asked why, they always give the same answer, "I love the game." I now totally understand where they are coming from.

Anyway, right after the selloff, we were right back at it. Not in the Section 8 game but the 'flipping game. You know, buy it for $100k, watch a couple of these "Flip That House" shows, and then sell the property for $200k. Too bad it hardly ever works out that way! The market was very hot when we first started doing flips, but it soon cooled. We made a pretty good buck off most of our investments and I can say we enjoyed working on them. Selling them was another story. You get your asshole buyers here and there that want you to put down a new floor or put in a new kitchen, or what have you. Then you get to hashing out a price. Nick and I always gave low offers and I expected that. What I didn't expect was a low offer, a laundry list of things they wanted fixed or added to the property, a five or six percent sellers assist, and finally they wanted a home inspector to come through the house and give us his list of repairs! Every property took at least 90 days to close or more and it was driving me nuts! No wonder, when Nick and I said, "We'll get the deal done in 30 days or less," the sellers came at us like crazy.

Another thing that was hard for us was not ripping out washer and dryer hook-ups, dishwashers, ceiling fans, etc. Once something is driven into your head it's hard to change. At first, Nick and I were walking around the property like Frankenstein saying must E-L-I-M-I-N-A-T-E, must E-L-I-M-I-N-A-T-E! But then we looked out the window and saw we weren't in Southwest Philly anymore. We should have been able to tell just by the quietness of the neighborhood, but we figured we'd look out the window again just to make sure.

Finally, the market started to soften up a little and, guess what? Prices in the city started to drop again! I guess the lure of cheap houses and guaranteed rent came calling us back. We purchased a 58 property package from a Philadelphia landlord and a 41 property package from another. I feel like I'm alive again! The landlord of the 58 property package could have sold when we did. Instead, he tried to hold out for a measly $1,000 more per property. Well, the negotiations blew up in his face. The potential buyer got tired of his demands and moved on. Pigs get fat and hogs get slaughtered! If someone is dangling five times more than what I paid for a property in front of my face, I'm grabbing it and running. He didn't and ended up selling them to us at a tremendous loss on his end.

Yep, we're going after it hard again! A lot of these Philadelphia landlords missed the boat and are now selling cheap, not to mention how many foreclosures that are popping up these days. This time we want to shoot for 500 properties. We feel like we can handle this amount and, if we can't, we now know how to 'flip'! Either way, we're gonna make a buck. When you love what you do and you're good at it, why give it up? It's like the old saying, "If you love what you do, you'll never have to work a day in your life."

I'm gonna tell you one thing I did with some of the money after selling off the properties; I bought my dad a new car. It was Father's Day and all of my brothers were over at my parent's house. I had them put a blindfold on my mom and dad and walk them out onto the front porch. I rolled up in a brand new Chrysler 300 and handed them the keys. It's a feeling that I, my brothers, or my parents will never forget!

Pop's new wheels!

My mom and dad are nearly 70-years-old and had never owned a new car. My dad worked for the city transportation (SEPTA) department for 35 years and always also worked a part-time job. He'd work eight hours for SEPTA, come home and eat dinner, then hit the door again to get to his part-time job. My mom took care of the five of us and also worked any job she could, not to mention keeping a spotless house, a cooked meal every morning and night, and would do about five loads of laundry a day.

If we needed money for a baseball glove, we got it. School clothes, no problem, Christmas and birthdays were never forgotten and always unbelievable! You name it and if we needed it, my parents always found a way to come through for each and every one of us. As a kid, you don't realize your dad is driving around in a piece of crap. You don't realize your parents never go out to dinner or that they don't buy anything for themselves. When you're older is when you realize, "Damn, the reason they didn't spend money on themselves is so we never did without."

I'm really not trying to get too personal here (although it sure seems like I am, huh). I am just trying to give you some motivation and inspiration. I did it and so can you. You can't wait for inspiration; you have to go after it with a club! I'm sure a lot of you also have great parents or someone that you would love to do something wonderful for. Staying idle and not taking risks won't get you to where you want to go in life. Being aggressive, jumping on smart deals, and working hard will get you there! If you stay focused, you'll not only be able to change your life for the better, you will also be able to change the life of people who are dear to you. It's not hard......you can do it!

CHAPTER 24

WRAPPING IT UP

A Note from the Mike on February 2020.

Hello again guys. It's Mike McLean and I'd like to thank you for your purchase of Volume 2. I hope you enjoyed it. Let me give you a little insight on how Volume 2 came about. After I released Volume 1 of the Section 8 Bible, I crossed my fingers and hoped for the best. Once I started seeing a good amount of sales, I knew that this "book thing" was going somewhere. Believe it or not, what I enjoyed more were the emails and reviews from people telling me how much they enjoyed the book and asking if there was going to be a Volume 2. This got me thinking and I said to myself, "What the hell, let's do it!"

I still had a ton of material in my arsenal, and do you know why? Because I was still making mistakes! All my mistakes lead to a good story and an even better lesson learned. What made Volume 2 even more fun to write was that I was so relaxed while writing it. I'd already developed my writing style, I had my fanbase in place, I didn't have to figure out how to publish the book. It was simply just time to sit down and write.

I enjoyed every minute of it. I can't describe to you how good it feels when I get a review on Amazon or an email from somebody who is an absolute reluctant reader and they tell me they have never finished reading a book until they picked up mine and they're looking forward to a Volume 2—I still get goosebumps!

I'm not trying to pump my own tires here; I just want to share with you what motivated me to write Volume 2. When I did commit to writing it, I didn't just want Volume 2 to be a follow up of Volume 1, I wanted it to be even better than Volume 1! I'd write and plug away sometimes until 4 o'clock in the morning, trying to make the book entertaining, informative, and of course, a little humorous. Long nights sitting at the dining room table writing about real estate, for me, there's nothing better. I hope that you found Volume 2 equally as, or even more, entertaining than Volume 1. If you did, again I ask that you give me a quick review on Amazon. The reviews really help!

Well, I hope by now that I've got you hooked and that you're ready to follow me onto the next step in the journey of Section 8 Landlording. The Section 8 Bible Volume 3 is ready to entertain you. LOL! I hope you enjoy it.

"THE GREATEST TOOL A LANDLORD CAN OWN IS AN AIRTIGHT LEASE"

After losing one too many eviction hearings, I realized that every lease I had purchased wasn't worth the paper it was printed on! So, I designed the Bulletproof Lease to protect me and my property.

My lease is packed with 41 terms and 14 addendums that protect you in easy-to-read English (so you won't have to worry about some fancy lawyer trying to use your words against you.) The addendums protect you more because the tenant must sign each and every one.

When I started out, I was using a lease that simply stated that the tenant would be responsible to replace any and all broken windows. Simple enough, right?

Wrong!

This one tenant had four broken windows that he refused to repair. His neighbors told me that his girlfriend had locked him out, and he went nuts. When I took him to court, the tenant claimed that kids playing baseball broke the windows—all four. Well, the judge bought the tenant's story and I was stuck with the tenant and the repair bill.

Now, my tenants must sign the "Broken Window Addendum." It's as simple as getting a signature, and I don't get any more broken window calls!

I'm currently using this exact lease on all 300 of my investment properties and I will never go back to a flimsy generic lease again.

I designed it, I use it, and I stand by it! It's your money and your investment, so play by your rules, not the tenant's! I guarantee that you will never think of using a generic lease again.

Get it at: www.shoptly.com/bulletprooflease

NOTE

Made in the USA
Las Vegas, NV
15 December 2023

82958359R00134